TECHNOLOGY AND COMMUNICATION IN AMERICAN HISTORY

D1248945

AMERICAN HISTORICAL ASSOCIATION – SOCIETY FOR THE HISTORY OF TECHNOLOGY

Historical Perspectives on Technology, Society, and Culture

A Series Edited by Pamela O. Long and Robert C. Post

Other Titles Published:

TECHNOLOGY AND COMMUNICATION
IN AMERICAN HISTORY

Gregory J. Downey

A Publication of the Society for the History of Technology
and the American Historical Association

GREGORY J. DOWNEY is a professor at the University of Wisconsin-Madison where he is also the director of the School of Journalism and Mass Communication. Downey received his B.S. and M.S. in computer science from the University of Illinois at Urbana-Champaign, an M.A. in liberal studies from Northwestern University, and a joint Ph.D. in the history of technology and human geography from Johns Hopkins University. He is the author of *Closed Captioning: Subtitling, Stenography, and the Digital Convergence of Text with Television* (Johns Hopkins University Press, 2008), and *Telegraph Messenger Boys: Labor, Technology, and Geography, 1850–1950* (Routledge, 2002).

COVER IMAGE: Alexander Graham Bell (1847–1922) poses for a photo along with a group of mustachioed admirers as he inaugurates long-distance telephone service between New York and Chicago in October 1892. Even though the telephone, like every other major invention, was the product of many minds, Bell will always reside securely in the American pantheon as "the" inventor. Division of Prints and Photographs, Library of Congress, Washington, D.C.

NOTE: Unless otherwise credited, all illustrations in this booklet are courtesy the Division of Prints and Photographs, Library of Congress.

SERIES EDITORS: Pamela O. Long, Robert C. Post

SERIES EDITOR-IN-CHIEF: Robert B. Townsend

LAYOUT AND DESIGN: Christian A. Hale

EDITORIAL ASSISTANCE: Liz Townsend

ACKNOWLEDGEMENT: The author would like to thank Pamela O. Long and Robert C. Post for their magnificent patience, enthusiasm, and guidance in the completion of this project.

© 2011 American Historical Association
ISBN: 978-0-87229-170-6

Published in 2011 by the American Historical Association. As publisher, the American Historical Association does not adopt official views on any field of history and does not necessarily agree or disagree with the views expressed in this book.

Library of Congress Cataloging-in-Publication Data:

Downey, Gregory John.

Technology and communication in American history / by Greg Downey.

p. cm. -- (Historical perspectives on technology, society, and culture)

"A publication of the American Historical Association and the Society for the History of Technology."

ISBN 978-0-87229-170-6

1. Communication and technology--United States--History. 2. Mass media and technology--United States--History. 3. Communication and traffic--United States--History. 4. Communication--Social aspects--United States--History. 5. Mass media--Social aspects--United States--History. I. American Historical Association. II. Society for the History of Technology III. Title.

P96.T422U634125 2011

302.20973--dc22   2010048305

TABLE OF CONTENTS

HISTORICAL PERSPECTIVES ON TECHNOLOGY, SOCIETY, AND CULTURE

SERIES INTRODUCTION

Technology reflects and shapes human history. Technology and history have been integral to one another from the establishment of neolithic farming and food-storage techniques to the development of metallurgy, weaving, printing, and electronics. The role of the stirrup in the Middle Ages, gunpowder in the thirteenth century, printing in the fifteenth, the steam engine in the eighteenth, factories in the nineteenth, and nuclear power in the twentieth are all subjects of an expansive scholarly literature. This literature spotlights many animated controversies about choices made among competing techniques for attaining the same end—whether automobiles would be powered by steam, electricity, or internal combustion, for example.

Yet the import of technology and its mutual interactions with society and culture have often been neglected in the high school, college, and even university curricula. When teachers unfamiliar with its rich historiography do consider technology, they all too often treat it as inert or determinate, lending their authority to the fallacy that it advances according to its own internal logic. Scholarly specialists now largely agree about what is called *social construction*: the idea that technologies succeed or fail (or emerge at all) partly because of the political strategies employed by "actors"—individuals, groups, and organizations—that have conflicting or complementary interests in particular outcomes. Most of them also agree that success or failure is contingent on inescapable physical realities, "that the human fabric depends to a large degree on the behavior of atoms," as the distinguished historian and metallurgist Cyril Stanley Smith put it. But there is no doubt that technological designs are shaped by ambient social and cultural factors, nor, indeed, that the shaping of technology is integral to the shaping of society and culture.

This booklet series, a joint venture of the Society for the History of Technology and the American Historical Association, draws on the analytical insights of scholars who address technology in social and cultural context. Some of them are concerned primarily with the relationship of technology to labor, economics, political structure, or the organization of production; sometimes their concern is with the role that technology plays in differentiating social status and the construction of gender; sometimes it is with *interpretive flexibility*—the perception that determinations about whether a technology "works" are contingent on the expectations, needs, and ideology of those who interact with it. Following from this is the understanding that technology is not intrinsically useful or even rational; capitalist ideology in particular has served to mask powerful nonutilitarian motives for technological novelty, among them kinesthetic pleasure, a sense of play, curiosity, and the exercise of ingenuity for its own sake, a phenomenon known as *technological enthusiasm*. As evidence of this, many inventions—from the mechanical clock during the Renaissance to the telephone and the automobile more recently—met only marginal needs at the outset. Needs with any substantial economic significance had to be contrived, thereby making invention the mother of necessity.

There are various definitions of technology. Sometimes it is defined as the way that "things are done or made," and this is a useful definition whenever one asks how things were done or made in a particular way in a particular context and then analyzes the implications of taking one path rather than another. Lynn White Jr., a historian who served as president of both the Society for the History of Technology and the American Historical Association, called this "the jungle of meaning." While the notion that technology marches of its own predetermined accord still has a strong hold on popular sensibilities, specialists in the interaction of technology, society, and culture now understand that it cannot do anything of the sort. Technology is not autonomous; rather, it is impelled by choices made in the context of circumstances in ambient realms, very often in the context of disputes over political power. Once chosen, however, technologies *can* exert a powerful influence on future choices. One only needs to consider the Strategic Defense Initiative, "Star Wars," which has been funded for decades not because it is actually feasible but because it provides partisans with effective political rhetoric.

Definitions of technology vary from one discipline to another. We believe that defining it as "the sum of the methods by which a social group provides itself with the material objects of their civilization" is sufficiently concrete without being too confining. It is important to specify the word *material*, for there are of course "techniques" having to do with everything from poetics to sex to bureaucratic administration. Some might go further and specify that "material" be taken to mean three-dimensional "things," and this seems satisfactory as long as one bears in mind that even an abstraction such as a computer program, or an idea for the design of a machine, or an ideology such as technocracy or scientific management is contingent upon its expression in tangible artifacts.

Prior to the twentieth century, issues that historians now frame in terms of the word *technology* were defined by the historical actors themselves in other terms. In his 1829 book titled *Elements of Technology*, the botanist Jacob Bigelow wrote that he used the term to encompass "the principles, processes, and nomenclature of the more conspicuous arts, particularly those which involve applications of science, and which may be considered useful." For some time, the word was used primarily in the context of technical education, a notable instance being the Massachusetts Institute of Technology, founded in 1861. For some time after that—and perhaps even today—it was not a term known to every culture. Technology still encompasses various actors' categories in diverse historical contexts, and that is part of the reason why contemporary scholars still define it variously. We believe that the complexity of definition, conceptual categories, and methodologies is instrumental in making the history of technology such a fruitful area of inquiry.

"Every generation writes its own history," said Carl Becker. In commissioning and editing the essays in these booklets, we have sought to have each one convey a broadly informed synthesis of the best scholarship, to outline the salient historiographical issues, and to highlight interpretive stances that seem persuasive to our own generation. We believe that the scholars represented in this series have all succeeded in integrating their inquiries with mainstream scholarship, and we trust that their booklets provide ample confirmation of this belief.

Pamela O. Long
Robert C. Post
Series Editors

THE POST-OFFICE DEPARTMENT.

The U.S. postal system with its cheap rates for printed material made it relatively inexpensive to send newspapers from one part of the country to another. Seen here is the U.S. Post Office Department in Washington, D.C., located on E Street N.W. between Seventh and Eighth. Construction was begun in 1825, and this engraving dates from 1851.

INTRODUCTION
COMMUNICATION, MEANINGS AND SOCIAL PURPOSES

By the end of the twentieth century, communication technologies of all sorts—from best selling children's books to mobile telephones, from portable music players to wide-screen televisions—were ubiquitous in American life. But only one of those technologies seemed to promise a "new economy" and an "information society" in a way that garnered not only consumer and media attention but also bipartisan government praise and fervent corporate speculation. Less than ten years after it was introduced to the public in the early 1990s, the computer-mediated "network of networks" known as the Internet—and its most user-friendly interface, the World Wide Web—had spawned a "dot. com" frenzy as businesses and schools, municipalities and individuals, all raced to claim what they hoped was valuable real estate in the new territory of cyberspace. To many, it seemed that all of our basic information and communication behaviors had changed overnight. Instead of seeking information in the library, now we "Googled" for "hits." Instead of reading that information sequentially, now we "surfed" through "hyperlinks." Instead of acting on that information locally, now we "blogged" before a worldwide (but often narrowly like-minded) audience. For a while, it seemed that communication technology had finally brought about "the death of distance," paradoxically producing a global society that one could consume from the comfort and isolation of one's own home.[1]

Soon into the new millennium, of course, the dot.com bubble burst, and with the terrorist attacks of September 11, 2001 (and the U.S. government's militarized response), attention turned away from virtual spaces of communication to the very material spaces of global extremism, urban warfare, and military occupation. The speed with which the "new media" of the World Wide Web became naturalized into the background of American political and cultural life demonstrates that the popularization of the Internet was by no means the end of American communication-technology history; it was merely the latest variation on an old theme.

Shortly after the nation's founding, both the national government and private enterprise committed to funding what they called "internal improvements," especially roads and canals. They realized that building a nation required the circulation of information, the movement of printed materials from across an ocean to the smallest town in the nation's interior.[2] During the first half-century, a period when the cost of long-distance travel was quite high because it entailed overnight stops with meals and lodging, sending printed material was relatively inexpensive. From 1793 to 1845, the postal rates set by Congress for newspapers

"*The Mountain Expressman,*" *a romanticized image of postal delivery in the American West. From Alonzo Delano,* Pen Knife Sketches, *published in Sacramento in 1853.*

were 1¢ for the first hundred miles and 1/2¢ for any distance beyond that, regardless of weight, and this especially favored the long-distance movement of large-circulation urban newspapers.[3] Individual cities would compete to be the first to augment their "natural advantages" (lakes and rivers for water transportation, valleys and plains for level roads) with "artificial advantages" (dredged harbors, canals, and, eventually, railroads). Transportation was fundamental to communication.[4]

By the late nineteenth century, by the time the nation was a hundred years old, steam power and electricity formed the basis of a new interlinked transportation and communication system, combining both material means, like sending letters via the railroad, and virtual means, like sending grain prices via the telegraph.[5] By the time it hosted the World's Columbian Exposition in 1893, the city of Chicago was a prime example of the benefits of such a system. Grain, meat, and timber all flowed in to the city from different regions of its hinterland, because regional producers found their highest price, easiest transit, and lowest risk in sending these commodities to Chicago rather than St. Louis or any other city. Appropriate structures, both physical and economic, were devised to handle these flows: animal slaughteryards, grain elevators, the Chicago Board of Trade, and the Montgomery Ward & Co. department-store empire, for example.[6] Together, both physical and virtual methods of communication facilitated a level of corporate command-and-control that enabled the first consolidation of nationwide firms (and gave rise to the labor organizations that challenged them).[7]

Shortly after 1900, new consumer tools such as the telephone and the Model T Ford were similarly hailed as components of an information infrastructure that would bring peace and prosperity not just to the United States, but to the entire globe. "Any device that enlarges one's environment and makes the rest of the world one's neighbors," wrote telephone innovator and advocate Amos Dolbear in 1900, "is an efficient missionary of civilization and helps to save the world from insularity where barbarism hides."[8] Two world wars later, it was upon the television and the computer that we pinned our hopes for a universally educated and automated leisure society. (By the mid-1950s, a majority of U.S. households had TVs and more than 1,000 U.S. firms were selling automated office systems).[9] Thus it is not surprising that by the early 1990s, at the end of a Cold War, we would turn those hopes (and not a few fears) to our latest communications infrastructure of the World Wide Web—a system born out of a process of "digital convergence" that promised to combine the best of print, telephone, and television together into a computerized "multimedia" resource. It was a future, according to MIT Media Lab founder Nicholas Negroponte in 1995, that would be "driven almost 100 percent by the ability of [a] company's product or services to be rendered in digital form."[10]

Over and over, we have celebrated our "new" media and tried to bury the "old," such that our very notions of media, modernity, and even "progress" have tended to unfold hand-in-hand.[11] The proponents of the latest communication technology—especially the producers and marketers of that technology—often invoke history in a teleological, deterministic sort of way. Local systems must give way to national systems, they might say (as long-distance telephone provider AT&T did in the early twentieth century), because it is a natural development.[12] Or, digital systems will replace analog systems, they might argue (as the movie industry did in the late twentieth century), because the one technology is functionally superior to the other.[13] And especially in recent history, public systems must give way to privatized systems, they might claim (as have critics of government funding for public broadcasting), because history shows there is no other choice.[14] Such pseudo-historical arguments tend to coincide with a particular vision of progress as necessarily centralized, rationalized, and privatized. No matter what logic is used—a geographical determinism of increasing reach, a technological determinism of improved functionality, or an economic determinism of greater efficiency—with communication technology, especially, history is invoked to consign previous ways of exchanging information to the junk-heap of obsolescence.

Photograph by Frances Benjamin Johnston of "The Great White Way" at the World's Columbian Exposition in Chicago in 1893. Johnston (1864–1952) was among the earliest woman photojournalists. Photo by Underwood and Underwood, 1909.

Amos Emerson Dolbear (1837–1910) was one of several inventors of devices important to the development of the telephone. Historic Collection, Digital Archives, Tufts University.

Yet digital culture has not displaced print culture; on the contrary, the World Wide Web is abundantly rich in written material. Web "pages" still draw their design aesthetic from the printed magazine; web "logs" (or "blogs") echo the essays and pamphlets of the alternative press; and even the digital video content of YouTube is indexed, debated, and disseminated using words. Though text is experienced in different ways from one generation to another, literacy still matters.[15] Neither has the supposedly "active" medium of the web displaced the allegedly "passive" pursuits of movie-going and television-viewing; rather, global media firms iterate their stories through each medium in turn, reducing the risk of new-media ventures by filling those channels with old-media content (something often called "synergy").[16] And as telephones and laptop computers both go "wireless," promising to allow individuals to work and learn and play from nearly anywhere, we bring our information and communication appliances into our cars, our coffeehouses, and our classrooms, still taking the time and effort to congregate with others, sometimes even more intensively and locally than we did before.[17] Old media and new media continue to coexist, even as the communication functions that they serve in society shift, split, and merge.[18]

Understanding the history of American communication technology, then, involves more than simply rehearsing a chronology of the old media of our grandparents' generation that led to the new media of our children's generation. Instead, we must attempt to connect the fundamental social processes of communication—exchanging information, enabling action at a distance, and participating in a shared symbolic culture—to several centuries of changing social norms, political-economic environments, and information infrastructures. Technologies matter, to be sure; they matter so much that historians of technology put them front and center in the histories they tell. But technologies are always produced and consumed, experienced and understood, embraced and

Stereograph of a young man listening to a radio set while reading. Underwood and Underwood, 1909.

rejected by human actors within social, political, and economic contexts.[19] This booklet, published through both the American Historical Association and the Society for the History of Technology, is meant to serve as an introductory (if idiosyncratic) guide to this broader field of culturally contextualized history of communication technology.

TELLING THE STORY OF COMMUNICATION TECHNOLOGY IN SOCIAL CONTEXT

The new and the old in 1950: television and the printed word communicate simultaneously in the same household.

One thing that makes communication technologies difficult to grasp historically is, paradoxically, their very ubiquity. Like technologies of transportation, power generation, and waterworks, communication technologies are by definition "infrastructure" technologies—whole systems meant to function reliably, invisibly, and perpetually in order to enable other social, political, and economic activities. We are forced to notice infrastructures when they break down. We are tempted to replace infrastructures when we believe we have exceeded their limits. But at the same time, we are often wedded to our older infrastructures because abandoning or devaluing them carries great risk. And the infrastructures of information and communication provide a special and self-referential case, because the very ability to discover, discuss, and debate the utility of technological infrastructures themselves presupposes a workable (and publicly accessible) technological system of social communication in the first place.[20]

Historians of technology have long experience in studying such "sociotechnical systems"—large-scale and long-lived assemblages not only of artifacts and machines, but of technical knowledge, bureaucratic procedures, political-economic structures, and, inevitably, human actors.[21] For example, from studying large technological industries like electrical power utilities, historians have found that sociotechnical systems nearly always involve particular kinds of entrepreneurial managers or "system builders" who attempt to bring a holistic vision of a new infrastructure into the world, often (in our capitalist political economy) for competitive market advantage. Yet our previous infrastructures are not abandoned easily, for they often embody a large measure of "technological momentum" both in the market position of their sponsoring firms and in the accumulated expertise of their daily laborers.[22] From studying the more decentralized technological practices of household labor, especially the often gender-segregated work of laundering and food preparation, historians have realized that the often anonymous actions of consumers can exert significant influence over the success or failure of a new sociotechnical system.[23] And from studies of a wide variety of cultural debates over the proper role of technology in society, from nuclear power to birth control, historians have revealed that just as sociotechnical systems are inevitably socially *produced* (brought into being by a myriad of social actors), they are also inevitably socially *constructed* (imbued with political and cultural meaning by social actors).[24]

But any history of communication technology needs to engage with a broad base of scholarship outside of technology studies as well. For example, from information and media studies comes nearly a century of research on the multiple and often contradictory ways that communication practices can be understood to "work" in society. In the days when "new media" meant broadcast radio, Harold Lasswell famously declared that communication could be defined as "Who says what in which channel to whom with what effect."[25] Later, when "new media" referred to color television, James Carey suggested that besides this "transmission" function (moving information from sender to receiver for some instrumental purpose, such as education, advertising, or social control), communication served a crucial "ritual" function (providing an opportunity to enact, reproduce, and sometimes challenge taken-for-granted cultural practices and shared cultural norms). In other words, communication could be understood broadly as "a symbolic process whereby reality is produced, maintained, repaired, and transformed."[26]

Such social transformations connected to communication are often most visible in the very sites we have long built to "overcome time with space" by bringing lots of people, products, and ideas together at a single place and at the same time: cities.[27] Popular writers have long asserted that new communication tools would result in the hollowing-out of traditional cities, spawning instead new decentralized rural or suburban forms of settlement with household-based production and consumption—what futurist Alvin Toffler called the "electronic cottage" in 1980.[28] However, empirical research during the last few decades shows both concentration and dispersion processes at work in the urban realm, often simultaneously. Urban theorist Manuel Castells sees these new "informational cities" as the nodes within a new "network society" where your chances of economic success depend on your ability to plug into flows of information as both a consumer and a producer.[29] Urban geographer Saskia Sassen points to a handful of "global cities" such as New York, Tokyo, and London that have already managed to pull in a disproportionate share of investment and control over global financial flows and decisions.[30] And urban planner William Mitchell sees both large and small cities as becoming "cities of bits," where electronic interactions will increasingly merge together with public urban spaces.[31] With over half of the world's population now living in urbanized areas, cities—suffused with communication technologies—are clearly here to stay.[32]

The discipline of geography helps reveal how communication technology—always intimately related to transportation technology—serves to produce new spatial and temporal relationships between countries, regions, cities, and even human bodies.[33] Geographer Donald Janelle has spoken of "time-space convergence" as a measure of "the rates at which places move closer together or further away in travel or communication time"—for example, the declining cost over time of a coast-to-coast telephone call in 1920 compared to the price of the same call today.[34] David Harvey suggests a similar idea with his term "time-space compression," where humans use technology of transport and communications to both broaden the space of social action and speed up the pace of that social action, especially political-economic processes such as the movement of financial capital or the deployment of military force. In this way, the production of new geographies through the deployment of new communication technologies shows that "the reorganization of space is always a reorganization of the framework through which social power is expressed."[35]

The Organization of This Booklet

Most efforts to make sense of this interdisciplinary history of communication have followed a sequential, technology-based periodization, tracing first the invention and then the naturalization of various large-scale communication systems in turn.[36] This booklet considers four such overlapping communication infrastructures:

Print communication and transportation: Text and image printed and preserved in books, magazines, and newspapers; circulated through networks of transportation (especially the state-funded postal service); and organized and preserved through institutions of education (schools and libraries). These forms date from the earliest European settlement of America to the present.

Networked interpersonal communication: From wired systems of telegraphs and telephones, to wireless systems of radio and cellular devices, these networks are used to transmit text, voice messages, and data in order to exert organizational control at a distance, using either analog or digital electrical impulses. They date from the mid-nineteenth century to the present.

Broadcast mass communication: The round-the-clock delivery of sound and image directly to individuals and households through radio and television channels—linked to a complementary industry of theatrical presentations and commodity recordings—casts listeners and viewers as a mass audience of citizens and consumers. These date from the early twentieth century to the present.

Computer-mediated communication: The convergence of all the previous forms of communication—text and image, message and control, audio and video—with digital, programmable, networked computer systems. These computer systems are increasingly becoming mobile, personal, and ubiquitous (especially for the most affluent and educated). They date from the mid-twentieth century to the present.

While this kind of organization by broad chronology and technology is useful, it can suggest a sort of technological determinism—both the idea that communication systems somehow unfold naturally or teleologically, one to the next, and the idea that each communication system has an inherent and universal effect (or "bias"), to which people must simply adapt. Communication scholar Marshall McLuhan expressed this point of view in the 1960s, speaking largely of television, with his playful assertion that "the medium is the message."[37] Contemporary historians of technology generally reject such determinism, favoring a more reciprocal or dialectical understanding that while we humans shape (and continually reshape) our technological environments for a myriad of social, political, and economic reasons, those technological environments in turn enable and constrain our actions and imaginations in significant ways.[38]

To better capture this complicated relationship between humans and their technologies, this booklet tells the story of these four communication infrastructures, and the historical periods in which they emerged, in two ways. It links each technology to a set of broader historical processes underway in each time period, and it considers several cross-cutting groups of historical actors whose choices and voices mattered to the way each technology developed. After all, communication infrastructures are inevitably created and deployed in order to extend human action and human knowledge across space and time, but for varied and often contradictory purposes of coordination, control, and cooperation, depending on historical circumstance. Each new "round" of communication innovation helps alter a society's very conceptions of distance and proximity, movement and mobility, place and space. But yesterday's innovations are soon regarded as today's bottlenecks. Calls for the reconstruction or reimagining of communication infrastructures can have many motivations, including economic efficiency, military dominance, social exclusion, and technological enthusiasm.

The key social, cultural, political, and economic processes tied to each technological infrastructure all involve the long transition to what might be called "modern society," and the gradual extension of that society to a global arena:

> **National integration:** Constructing a national polity, economy, and community through print communication and transportation in the nineteenth century, especially under state-directed investments in "internal improvements" connecting flows of people, goods, and ideas among regions, states, and cities.

> **Urbanization and industrialization:** Confronting the "control challenge" of rapid economic and social growth through point-to-point electronic communication around the turn of the twentieth century, especially in response to the new energy abundance provided by fossil fuels and electrification.

Mass production and consumption: Mobilizing new methods of broadcast network communication to create a mass culture and manufacture consent throughout the twentieth century, including the development of whole new industries of expert media manipulation and product marketing.

Global economic restructuring: Responding to the new challenges of transnational competition and neoliberal governance through computer-mediated communication at the turn of the twenty-first century, in what observers have labeled a new "post-industrial," "postmodern," or "network" society.

The cross-cutting groups of actors involved with each technological infrastructure include those who bring new communication infrastructures to life, those who adapt existing communication infrastructures for new uses, and those who debate the value of allowing our social processes of production, consumption, education, and citizenship to become mobilized through communication infrastructures:

The democratic state, especially as a regulator and sponsor of the capitalist market in deploying communication infrastructures. In each of our four time periods, state support for the development of communication infrastructure (for economic goals) becomes entwined with military support for the development of communication infrastructure (for strategic goals). Innovation is often incubated in (or contracted to) public, non-profit academic settings and then transferred to (or appropriated by) private, for-profit corporate settings.

The capitalist market, focused on corporate accumulation strategies as the motivation for the development of communication technology. Firms attempt to adopt (or promote) new communication technology in order to achieve a competitive advantage in coordinating their activities over time and space—producing commodities faster, extending their markets, or intensifying their advertising. Yet these same firms often find it difficult to inaugurate an entirely new communication infrastructure on their own, without some sort of state subsidy, sponsorship, or regulation. And even after a new communication technology is successfully brought to bear on accumulation, the paradox remains that once all competitors have adopted a new communication technology, it might cease to provide competitive advantage.

The communication users, whose adoption and innovation are both key to the success of any new communication technology. Technologies that never find a consumer market stand little chance of influencing historical development. The risks of failure are high, so new technologies are often cast as upgrades to the old, promising consumers the ability to do whatever they were doing before—only better, faster, and cheaper. But over and over again, consumers of new communication technologies have demonstrated a surprising ability to use and adapt these devices and systems for unforeseen purposes. And sometimes these novel uses—especially when rooted in user groups outside of the mainstream, such as youth culture or minority culture—can incite social fear and moral outrage even as they generate new markets and new ideas.

The communication laborers, whose work and expertise are required for any communication revolution, not only in the initial development and deployment of a new information infrastructure, but also in the daily reproduction and use of that infrastructure. Since the industrial revolution hit the shores of North America, the United States has faced again and again the question of whether technology should be used to "augment" human action or to "automate" human action. As information technologies have become mechanized, electrified, and digitized, the form and content of much human communication itself has shifted from live enactment, performance, and service to scripted, produced, and recorded commodity. Yet each attempt to control or co-opt labor through communication involves a reassertion of new forms of labor, often at the boundaries between old communication systems and new.

What this combined focus on technological infrastructures, social processes, and historical actors illustrates is that, throughout American history, new communication technologies have always interacted with the old in complicated and often contingent ways, rather than simply replacing each other in turn. Technologically "superior" forms of communication do not simply make obsolete the "inferior" ones; rather, new and old technological systems both cooperate and compete within a society's ever-changing communication environment. Just as the rise of television in the 1950s did not destroy print, radio, and film, but instead pressured them to recast their social roles and target audiences, the shift of so many of our communications activities to the Internet today will not simply destroy print culture, point-to-point communication systems, or broadcast networks, but, rather, will allow us to reframe them in ways that will, no doubt, later be seen as "inevitable" and "natural" even though they are anything but.

1

PRINT COMMUNICATION AND TRANSPORTATION: CONSTRUCTING A NATIONAL MARKET AND AN IMAGINED COMMUNITY

The history of communication technology as a whole could be thought of as the slow and uneven movement from orality to literacy as described by the Jesuit scholar Walter Ong. Whether printed on paper or recorded on electromagnetic tape, the very notion that information and communication are "assimilated to things," captured and transmitted "out there" as Ong put it, implies the existence of some sort of technological infrastructure for meaning-making that is fundamentally different from that required by a culture operating through purely oral traditions.[1] Such a conception does hold risks, however. If one follows anthropologist Jack Goody in seeing the distinction between oral or literate modes as one of the key factors, together with agriculture and urbanization, in the development of modern social structure, does this reinforce imperialist or racist ideas of progress and superiority through technology and bureaucracy?[2] Media critic Neil Postman put forth a thesis similar to Ong's to argue that a society dependent on television was substituting an inferior visual literacy of entertainment distraction for the previous textual literacy of evidence-based argument; would we say the same about today's hybrid text-and-image World Wide Web?[3] As writing scholar Deborah Brandt has argued, literacy in this sense is not an unchanging, ahistorical category, but a concept tied both to a society's technological infrastructure and to its political-economic environment. A high-school graduate in the deindustrialized economic landscape of present-day Detroit may objectively operate at a higher

This photograph depicting a vocational education course for African Americans is indicative of the importance of printing as a medium of communication at the turn of the twentieth century. The location is Claflin University, Orangeburg, South Carolina, c.1899.

level of literacy than his or her parents and grandparents ever did; however, that level of literacy still might not help in finding a job.[4] Treating the technologies of language in an overly determinist way, then, ignores the fact that any oral, written, or even visual communication infrastructures that emerge over time do not simply replace each other sequentially, but, rather, they coexist and coevolve together.

The first such infrastructure to consider in the history of American communication had at its center the printing press, inherited from the European Renaissance and Reformation. The printing press as historical artifact has been heralded by historians as a revolutionary "agent of change" through its inspiration to democratization and exploration, and it has also been debunked as merely an evolutionary moment in the larger history of print culture that began (and continued) with hand-copied books, papers, and other written materials.[5] Whether revolutionary or evolutionary, however, and even though the introduction of moveable type was located in western Europe with Gutenberg in the early modern period, the technological precondition of sophisticated papermaking had itself spread to Europe from Chinese and Muslim cultures in the previous centuries.[6] And regardless of the technology used to store and move text, one might take the audience's point of view, rather than the author's, and speak of broad cultural shifts in reading practices and meanings (from narrated or public reading to silent or individual reading, for example) as revolutionary in their own right.[7]

In the early years of exploration, conquest, and colonization in North America, this infrastructure was defined by printed text and image—largely originating in the commercial and religious institutions of western Europe—as it moved across the ocean on sailing ships, across the colonies on horse-drawn wagons, and across the community through human hands. Formal systems were developed for disseminating, organizing, and preserving these artifacts, texts, and images, including religious schools, colonial colleges, and commercial and subscription libraries. It was in institutions like these that, as library historian Thomas Augst put it, "the seemingly private and solitary nature of reading itself becomes a feature of social life." In the colonial period, private-membership library projects were an elite statement of Enlightenment goals, setting forth as social ideals the processes of learning and reflection (even if those ideals failed to live up to the reality of a slaveholding

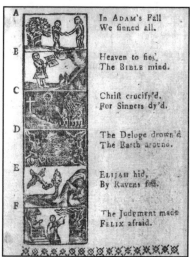

Children were taught reading and religious precepts in primers such as this one from 1773.

colonial economy that largely restricted public literary participation to propertied white males). At the same time, commercial circulating libraries (Augst likens them to the movie-rental stores of today) traded not in works of political philosophy, but in popular novels and entertainments, catering to less affluent readers (and even to women).[8]

Underpinning all of this print culture production, circulation, and consumption was a growing awareness in American society of the importance of print literacy—the ability to decode the printed word and image, to make meaning from these material artifacts. Historian

In colonial America, libraries made the seemingly solitary activity of reading "a feature of social life." Here, a Historic American Buildings Survey photo of 1970 shows the Redwood Library, Newport, Rhode Island, as it looked when constructed in 1749.

Richard Brown has argued that it was the widespread commitment to Protestant Christian ideals and practices that resulted in a nascent society where "European settlers in colonial America—British, German, and French alike—were more widely literate than the peoples of France or Germany, and at least as literate as those of Great Britain."[9] Harvey Graff locates this preponderance of literacy in a more complicated "migratory selectivity" among those who traveled to the American colonies of the seventeenth century: "persons more likely to be literate for religious, familial, occupational, demographic, geographic, or economic reasons, and/or from places with higher-than-average rates of literacy, were more likely to migrate over the long transatlantic distance."[10]

The first volume of the new multivolume *History of the Book in America*, subtitled *The Colonial Book in the Atlantic World*, sheds some more detailed light on early American literacy rates and reading practices.[11] Historians attempting to measure the rate of "signature literacy" (the ability to formally sign one's name) in New England found that it had reached 90 percent among white men by 1790, with a

A romanticized watercolor by H. L. Stephens depicts a black man reading the Emancipation Proclamation by candlelight in 1863. Before the Civil War, African American slaves found many more opportunities to learn to read than to write.

somewhat lower level for "urban women and those from wealthier families." Race was also a factor in literacy rates, especially for enslaved African Americans in the South, although "the possibilities for learning how to read far exceeded the possibilities for learning how to write, for no slave owner wanted slaves to be able to communicate with each other or fashion documents that could allow them to escape or move about."[12] As for the literacy experiences of the previous inhabitants of the territories claimed by the European colonists, as historian David D. Hall notes, "the project of converting the Indians to Christianity," undertaken by missionaries of many Protestant and Catholic groups, involved the use of "preaching, books, schools for introducing the Indians to literacy in their own languages and in those of the Europeans, and communities or settlements" for forced "civilization" efforts. The "republic of letters" that resulted from these unique conditions of restricted literacy plus print availability may not have encompassed the whole of colonial society, but it did enable "a middling social and cultural space in which many texts seem to have circulated widely."[13]

PAPER, PRINTING, AND PUBLISHING

Massachusetts had a printing press by 1630, but for decades the lack of affordable paper, skilled labor, and a paying market meant that colonial printing was dominated by three main types of clients: government, merchants, and the church. By 1756, almanacs and newspapers made up about half of the press runs in Boston. With only a few presses in Massachusetts, Connecticut, New York, and Philadelphia, colonists had to import most of their printed matter. After 1776, as historians Ronald and Mary Zboray write, "Independence brought countless calls for a national literature, answered haltingly by a few belles-lettrists, but more successfully by numerous schoolbook, geography, and dictionary authors."[14] But in the early American Republic, for many years, "printed goods were scarce and expensive commodities, almost always intended to serve the needs of magistrates, merchants, and the learned professions, as well as the pleasures of the gentry."[15]

Photograph of a painting by Charles E. Mills, c. 1914, of Benjamin Franklin's print shop. The scene is imaginary, although Franklin (1706–90) did own one of the most successful printing establishments in colonial America.

Through the early 1800s, books published in Europe—and particularly English-language books from London—dominated the commercial publishing trade from history to law, science to religion. Here printed communication relied on oceangoing transportation across the Atlantic, where everything from problems of credit and payment to vagaries of winds and weather combined for an average order-to-delivery cycle of more than a year. Domestic printers faced great risk when they tied up capital in publishing books that might not sell (even the London booksellers often dumped unprofitable works on the American market). By the 1830s a domestic publishing industry had begun to emerge, however, just as new production and transportation technologies such as the steam press

Engraving of a papermaking vat from J. E. A. Smith's A History of Paper, published in Holyoke, Mass., in 1882.

and the railroad emerged to allow these ventures to reap economies of scale by selling books across the nation, reducing the average price of a book to about a dollar in 1850 (an average worker's daily wage). Surveys in Ohio in the 1840s and 1850s suggested that about half of all households there owned books; often these were Christian religious texts, such as those published by the American Bible Society and the American Tract Society.[17] Print was increasingly visible in the public sphere as well; David Henkin writes of antebellum New York City as "a city plastered with written words," decorating not just buildings, poles, and physical infrastructure of all sorts, but carried on the backs of sandwich-board laborers as well, making public and ubiquitous a new urban and national language of persuasion and politics.[18]

In the colonial period, paper and binding accounted for two-thirds of a book's cost, resulting in domestically printed books that were small, dense, and "dingy."[19] But paper-making in the nineteenth century moved from a skilled craft to an industrial process as did so many other production trades subject to new forms of organization and mechanization. Historian Judith McGaw, in her study of the Berkshire paper industry between the 1820s and the 1880s, found that workmen who once simply called themselves "paper makers" later identified with individual, specialized production roles like "machine tender" or "assistant finisher." Such jobs, still often highly skilled, were subject to greater speed-up, longer work days, and greater danger. Belt-driven machinery could snag clothing and pull workers in; mechanized cutting tools took digits and limbs; steam-powered pipeworks could leak or explode; and the lard-oil lubricants, mixed with the smoke of kerosene lanterns and the water vapor evaporating from the drying paper, made for a dusty, damp, and foul working atmosphere.[20]

The wider availability of paper, through changes in industrial work, helped usher in a new meaning of handwriting, through changes in office work. In the clerical professions of the late nineteenth century, the style and uniformity of one's script might be related to one's status or gender; whether one wrote neatly or

Two stenographers at work in 1903 at the Leland & Faulconer Manufacturing Co., a Detroit foundry and machine shop involved in the early production of automobile engines.

poorly might be thought to imply much about character or trustworthiness.[21] On the other hand, the speed of one's ability to record the spoken word through script—the practice of stenography—might be interpreted differently depending on the social situation of that labor: A supposedly widely educated and incorruptible male courtroom reporter was valued more highly than a vocationally trained, low-waged office steno girl. But even these gender and status divisions in the workplace, which increasingly depended on the production, recording, organization, and retrieval of internal communications in printed form, were complicated by the introduction of technological fixes like typewriters, dictaphones, and stenotypes.[22] Sometimes male managers adopted these new tools to change a division of print-production labor, but other times they might refuse to use such tools as a way of preserving their authority or the value of their mental labor time. Whole industries, like business clerking in the late nineteenth century and courtroom stenography in the mid-twentieth century, eventually shifted demographically in a "feminization" from male-dominated to female-dominated workforces (though males still tended to wield managerial power and reap higher wages even as their numbers declined).[23]

Newspapers, Journalism, and Community

The increasingly timely production and circulation of mechanized print through broad communities of readers was best exemplified by the industrialization of the newspaper and magazine industry through the nineteenth century.[24] Communication historian David Nord called the decades from 1820 to 1850 "the take-off stage for daily newspapers," with the number of daily papers in America rising tenfold from 24 to 254 during that period. One reason for this was the so-called "penny press" strategy—best exemplified by the *New York Herald* as it was first published by James Gordon Bennett in 1835—of minimizing cost per copy, maximizing readership, and commanding the greatest possible advertising revenue.[25] Much of this circulation was quite literally handled by the Post Office. Historian Richard John reports that "In 1832, newspapers generated no more than 15 percent of total postal revenue, while making up as much as 95 percent of the weight." This cross-subsidy for the delivery of news was paid for by merchants doing business through the mail. And an interesting side effect of news delivery through the post was that even those who could not read could often listen to an amateur narration of the week's events as long as they spent time at the local post office.[26]

But more than just the number of newspapers and the size of their audience changed during this period. The new economic landscape of news production and distribution was coupled with a political shift. Overtly partisan papers began to give way to seemingly "objective" (but often just as sensationalist) news properties. As Gerald Baldasty argues, "Reflecting business imperatives and publishers' desire for profits, news became a commodity—a product shaped and marketed for profit."[27] Such connections between newspaper publics and national politics have been puzzled over in recent decades through two

The New York Herald *best exemplified the "penny press" strategy of minimizing cost per copy, maximizing readership, and bringing in the largest possible advertising revenue.*

main frameworks. Social theorist Jürgen Habermas has proposed the idea of the "public sphere," today interpreted as any social site where rational debate about the reach of the market and the state might proceed, in an open and civil manner, largely outside the controlling grip of the market and the state.[28] In a related but distinct thesis, historian Benedict Anderson has pointed to the "imagined communities" created through the shared consumption of cultural media (especially daily news) as necessary complements to functioning urban, regional, and national political-economic units.[29] Both thinkers, and those who have built on their work in new ways in recent years, point to the power of the press in shaping political history.

A linotype machine, the invention of Ottmar Mergenthaler (1854–99), a German clockmaker who immigrated to the United States in 1872. Beginning in the 1880s, Mergenthaler's continuous improvements to his invention precipitated great change in the printing industrry.

That power was, and still is, rooted in both technology and labor. The technology of newspaper-making shifted dramatically after the 1860s, as the Civil War, westward expansion, and steam-powered industrialization helped foster an increased demand for paper. Using wood-pulp cellulose rather than the previous raw material of rags, the newspaper industry was restructured to operate on

In 1902, linotype operators in the composing room of the New York Herald. *Linotypes displaced highly skilled typesetters after the 1880s.*

cheap newsprint. All of this printing of text for books and newspapers was accomplished by a skilled social and technical division of typesetting labor that occurred around the clock and often in hidden, poorly-ventilated workshops. The fastest compositors often worked for the big daily newspapers, belonged to the International Typographic Union, and even competed in typesetting speed contests. But after the 1880s the Linotype machine could set lines of type much faster—the number of newspaper copies sold each day increased tenfold from 1870 to 1900—and these skilled men and women of the print shop all but disappeared.[31]

By the turn of the twentieth century, the industrialized newspaper was a staple of urban life—and the 1920 U.S. census revealed that urban life was, for the first time, the daily social world of a majority of Americans. The *New York Daily News* was a good example of the cutting edge of newspaper technology when it emerged in 1919. Started by one of the grandsons of the inventor of the McCormick reaper, this was the first "tabloid" paper: with a smaller size, it used less paper, was easier to read when people were crowded together on public transportation, and lent itself better to large headlines and photos rather than dense columns of text.[32] Such newspapers as fixtures of urban communication technology embodied two somewhat contradictory ideals, according to media historian Michael Schudson. In the "story" ideal, "The news serves primarily to create, for readers, satisfying aesthetic experiences which help them to interpret their own lives and to relate them to the nation, town, or class to which they belong." This ideal was targeted more to middle- and working-class readers, as epitomized by Joseph Pulitzer's *New York World*. But the "information" ideal was instead "associated with fairness,

The tabloid newspaper emerged after World War I, smaller overall but with large headlines and large photos rather than dense columns of text. Here, the New York Daily News *for January 13, 1928, reports that Ruth Brown Snyder and Henry Judd Gray were executed in the electric chair at Sing Sing Prison for the murder of Ruth's husband Albert.*

objectivity, scrupulous dispassion" in the hope that "the facts it provides are un-framed." This competing ideal, epitomized by the *New York Times* under Adolph Ochs, was targeted to the "educated middle class."[33]

These large, successful newspapers tell only part of the story, however. Historians of print culture are paying increasing attention not only to the mainstream texts that circulated through middle-class households, but also to the many subcultures made visible as particular communities of print.[34] Unfortunately, the most common way that many minority groups—especially African Americans—were made visible in print culture was through stereotypes of text and image. Not coincidentally, print stereotyping went hand-in-hand with print exclusion, with political and economic segregation and prejudice keeping more than 90 percent of blacks in the antebellum era illiterate. But even in an African American community torn by slavery there was nearly always some thread of print culture—often tied to institutions supporting reading such as small clubs, mutual aid societies, or churches—and as the technological and economic means of publishing and circulation widened, these groups were increasingly able to represent their own identities and interests in print, both for their own communities and for the mainstream.[35]

PRODUCING ILLUSTRATION AND CONSUMING IMAGE

The burgeoning print culture of the nineteenth century was not just comprised of text. By the mid-1850s, building on L.J.M. Daguerre's "daguerreotype" chemical photographic process of two decades earlier, photography was a bustling business. It was by no means an amateur pursuit, however. As Reese Jenkins has written, a professional photographer of the mid-nineteenth century needed to be chemist, artist, and printer all in one. First, the photographer prepared and applied the "collodion," a solution of photosensitive silver salts, to a glass-plate negative. Then, working quickly (because as it dried, the collodion became less effective), the photographer set up the exposure with the camera and fixed the image onto the negative plate. Finally, the photographer produced the final print on special photosensitive paper, also self-prepared. Such a profession was as much about facility with technology and materials as it was about scene and composition.[36]

Within this very time-sensitive and highly skilled labor process, amateur photographer George Eastman offered a twofold innovation in the late 1870s. First, he developed a system for creating a photosensitive chemical plate that was "dry" rather than wet (once prepared, it would remain useful for months). And second,

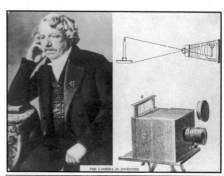

Louis Jacque Mandé Daguerre (1787–1851), inventor of the photographic process that bears his name.

In this daguerreotype, an unidentified young woman holds a daguerreotype case. The daguerreotype, most often a portrait, was the basis of a bustling business involving a complicated set of skills.

he secured the funding, expertise, and patents to mechanize the process of producing these dry plates for sale in large numbers to other photographers. By the late 1880s, the original Eastman Dry Plate Company had connected with enough other innovators and investors to put forth a new form of roll film and become the Eastman Dry Plate and Film Company. The first production models of their new "Kodak" camera, with a hundred exposures on a pre-loaded roll of film for $25, appeared in 1888 to wide acclaim. As Jenkins describes, "The novice photographer had only to point the camera toward the desired subject and 'push the button.' When he had exposed the film, he had only to return the camera to the factory where for $10 the film was removed and replaced with a fresh roll of film and the exposed film processed."[37]

Even before the camera became commonplace in the toolkits of hobbyists and journalists, however, audiences had become accustomed to the marriage of visual culture with print culture: labor-intensive wood-engraved artists' renderings of stories and events filled popular Gilded Age weekly periodicals like *Frank Leslie's Illustrated Newspaper*. By the end of the nineteenth century, mass-circulation magazines competed with each other on the basis of the changing four-color cover illustrations sported by each issue. A new visual vocabulary circulated through print media, revealing a diverse world to many locally bound readers. But the way

George Eastman's invention of a photosensitive dry plate enabled the creation of the Kodak camera, which allowed novice photographers to take pictures. Here, in 1917, a girl snaps a "Kodak" of her doll.

this world was represented in photography—a technology that, as Richard Dyer has argued, was itself developed under the assumption that it would always be a light-skinned "white" face that was to be captured on film—often acted to reinforce those stereotypes of class, race, and gender that seemed to sell the most copies.[38]

From the hand-drawn reproductions of Mathew Brady's Civil War photographs in the 1860s to the halftone reproductions of urban squalor captured by pioneering photojournalist Jacob Riis in *How the Other Half Lives* in the 1890s, the dissemination of photography in the nineteenth century not only brought a new urgency to the visual practices of journalism, but also opened up a new space for producing meaning from visual imagery.[39] For example, Marc Olivier has recently explored the history of Kodak's 99¢ "Brownie" instant camera, first introduced in 1900, arguing that the strategy of naming it after the invisible, magical forest sprites of Scottish folklore was more than a simple marketing gimmick: "Eastman's conflation of the product with its commercialized mythic namesake was a campaign to portray snapshot photography as a phenomenon both modern and magic, one that fulfilled the primitive urge toward visual communication."[40] Critics and consumers began to debate: Were photographs an artistic medium of expression, guided by a human point of view, or a naturalistic medium of simple collection, with a neutral, objective vision?[41]

Frank Leslie's Illustrated *combined visual images and print in imaginative ways. Here, on the issue for July 7, 1877, a wood engraving from a sketch by Harry Ogden depicts "the evasion of the liquor law in Colorado Springs." Four men are drinking beer being passed to them through a small door in a wall.*

MOVING PRINT ACROSS SPACE AND TIME

For all of these currents of print culture, however—European books and American newspapers, personal letters and business correspondence, magazines and photographs—the post office was the crucial transportation conduit, itself an overland communication system traveling at the speed of human-, animal-, or steam-driven labor. Thomas Jefferson had argued in an address to Congress in 1806 that taxpayers and legislators should direct federal budget surpluses to "public education, roads, rivers, canals, and such other objects of public improvement as it may be thought proper to add to the

Photograph by Jacob Riis of "unauthorized immigration lodgings" in a New York City tenement, c. 1890. Riis (1849–1914) was a crusading journalist and documentary photographer. The dissemination of photography in the nineteenth century brought new urgency to the visual practices of journalism and opened up a new space for producing meaning from visual imagery.

constitutional enumeration of federal powers," because "new channels of communication will be opened between the states, the lines of separation will disappear, their interests will be identified, and their union cemented by new and indestructible ties."[42] Such "public improvements" linking eastern coastal cities with the western frontier of resource extraction and immigrant expansion, even with all the local political controversy and private economic speculation they often generated, were nevertheless considered the proper and natural undertaking of the federal government.[43]

Different historians of the post office have emphasized different cultural and political-economic ramifications of this sociotechnical system. While Richard John has focused on the nation-building processes of political information exchange through the government-subsidized flow of local newspapers and polemical pamphlets, David Henkin has looked to the more prosaic nature of the private and personal letter, arguing that individual and institutional mobility across the nation demanded a restructuring in postal rates that would normalize the hidden flow of correspondence required to undertake family or business action at a distance.[44] As the main channel of cultural distribution, however, the mail also became a main target of cultural criticism in early American debates over media morality—especially after the 1870s when the railway mail service streamlined cross-country mail delivery and began to allow for a national mass mailing market. Religious groups and freethinker societies, labor groups and suffrage organizations, accused the post office of supporting such alleged social evils as the spread of pornography, the distribution of lotteries, and the dissemination of birth-control advice.[45]

A montage from Frank Leslie's Illustrated, November 6, 1888, shows "The Railway Mail Service—Methods of Distributing and Delivering the Mail." Newspapers relied on the post office for wide distribution.

Besides looking at the movement of print over space, historians must consider the preservation of print over time. A focus on libraries reveals the contradictions and conflicts inherent in a state-supported but privately profitable print culture that is meant to enlighten readers into responsible republican citizens, but depends for its circulation on a mass aesthetic appeal that must go beyond the idealized norms of high culture.[46] Congress had authorized its own library shortly after the nation was founded, but it would be some time before this Library of Congress would take on the role of setting cataloging, copyright, and collections standards for the rest of the nation.[47] Meanwhile, the research literature collected by the first large urban libraries of the mid-nineteenth century was paralleled by a burgeoning popular press as literacy rates rose in America. The same pre-Civil War technological scale-up of papermaking and printing that allowed the publication of the penny paper or the sober political tract enabled the circulation of ephemeral, festive, and often shock-

The Library of Congress was established in 1800. Construction of the present building was begun in 1892 and completed in 1897. This photo shows the Main Reading Room as it loooked between 1930 and 1950.

ing popular novels, gift books, and oversized magazines to a growing body of literate (and largely female) readers.[48] Late-nineteenth-century librarianship wrestled with both the public-interest arguments for free library provision of quality literature for the working classes, and the moral panics over censoring and curtailing the purchase of the now corporate-produced pulp literature that made up the chosen reading material of those same masses.[49]

Today, the greatest concern for moving print across time seems to be not the fear of wide public readership, but the protection of narrow private profit. As cultural historian Siva Vaidhyanathan has argued, the understanding of all information and communication artifacts and transmissions as "intellectual property"—to be defended, by definition, against "theft" and "piracy" at all costs—is relatively new. Although debates over copyright dating back to the eighteenth century did indeed consider the rights of authors to control their "property"—under what conditions of time and trade that authors should have monopoly control over written works that they created—these debates also involved careful attention to the public's rights to access, parody, and benefit from written works as a sort of intellectual commons (what we might call "remixing" today).[50] Media scholar Tarleton Gillespie brings this history up-to-date by noting that recent debates over copyright have slowly shifted from the pursuit of policy remedies to the reliance on the technological fix: Today, rights owners simply ensure, through hardware chips and software keys, that a corporate-sold DVD cannot physically be duplicated when one wires a corporate-sold DVD player to a corporate-sold digital video recorder. Through the accumulation and acceptance of such individual "digital rights management" technologies, over time, the entire sphere of cultural production threatens to become more a place for corporate profit than a site for creative debate.[51]

All of these interrelated concerns—the circulation of words and pictures over space and time, the question of the place of the press in public life, and the debate over the profitability of commodified intellectual property versus the fair and free use of a shared intellectual commons—remain with us after the turn of the millennium, even as the print culture of paper technology seems to make way for the digital culture of computer technology. Having been woven into our society over a span of centuries, the sociotechnical system for communication through print is unlikely to evaporate overnight. The modest written word, with its enduring metaphor of the page and the book, and its labor demands for both seriousness of argument and playfulness of style, lives on in the most high-tech of hand-held wireless devices for networked digital communication.

2

NETWORKED INTERPERSONAL COMMUNICATION: SEARCHING FOR CONTROL IN GOVERNMENT, INDUSTRY, AND SOCIETY

If investments in the culture of printed communication succeeded in bringing an expanding geography of disparate regions, political units, immigrant populations, and business actors together into a new nation by the early nineteenth century, it was not long before this same nation of print-based (and travel-tied) communication was encountering a new set of continent-wide crises enabled by that same success. First were the military demands of ending a Civil War in the 1860s, tied not only to the movement of troops and supplies over the new transportation technology of railroads, but also to the coordination of such movement over the new communication technology of telegraphs. But even through the early years of Reconstruction there arose new political demands, like conducting an accurate and legitimate census of the growing and urbanizing population as demanded by the Constitution—a problem of print, movement, and calculation that seemed to absorb as many labor resources as the government could afford to throw at it.[1] And in the late-nineteenth-century Gilded Age of economic crisis and expansion, the logistical demands of new coast-to-coast firms in getting raw materials to factory and finished products to market—such as those faced by food giant G. F. Swift in linking farmers, meatpackers, and retailers across a continent-wide market for cheap protein—seemed to threaten the very economic foundations of the nation.[2]

America seemed to be facing what historian James Beniger called a "crisis of control."[3] How could urban bureaucracies based on face-to-face communication be stretched out across the time and space of a whole continent? How could large sums of capital and accurate information on prices move quickly and safely from a buyer on one coast to a seller on another? How could centralized corporate management keep

Military Telegraph Operators, Headquarters, Army of the Potomac, Bealeton, Virginia, August 1863.

an ever-growing and ethnically diverse labor force under surveillance and control? And how could those same laborers ever hope to organize across field and factory for their common interests against capital? What made this crisis of control all the more urgent was the fact that it came together with another crisis, a crisis that historian Stephen Kern has termed a "crisis of abundance."[4] Sometimes termed the "second industrial revolution," large firms were now able to liberate huge amounts of energy from newly harnessed fossil fuel sources, coal and oil, circulating this power through nascent electrical power and lighting systems to extend the spatial reach and the temporal length of the industrial working day like never before.

The control of such abundance became dependent on both the speed and the reach of communication. The multimodal transportation network of roads, canals, and rails required the rapid movement of price information in order to efficiently move people and goods; it also required the careful coordination of logistical information in order to avoid spectacular disasters and delays (especially when many rail lines used a single track for traffic in both directions). As JoAnne Yates demonstrates for the railroad, manufacturing, and chemical industries, the introduction of new production and distribution technologies was accompanied by the rationalization of management techniques—especially through internal communication technologies—where previously informal routines were formalized and systematized under the buzzword of "efficiency."[5] Similarly, William Cronon has demonstrated how in key farming and extractive industries—corn, timber, and hogs—the relationship between a metropolis and its hinterland, connecting natural resources, processed goods, labor power, and financial capital, grew to be mediated by new flows of mechanical movement and electronic information, and managed by middlemen like banks and brokers.[6]

From the mid-nineteenth century to the mid-twentieth, then, a new series of overlapping and interlocking communication infrastructures emerged: point-to-point "networked" communication systems. Starting with the railroad and the telegraph, which conveyed the content of textual print culture in both physical and virtual forms, respectively, these new electromechanical networks eventually expanded to convey sound and voice as well, through the wired telephone and the wireless radio. It was, as one historian argued, a "second information revolution" to accompany the second industrial revolution.[7]

BUILDING TEXT AND VOICE NETWORKS THROUGH THE MARKET AND THE STATE

The story of the innovation, deployment, and naturalization of first the telegraph and then the telephone network is often told as a classic case of rational technological progress. Although Samuel Morse is credited with bringing the technology of the telegraph to America, it was his partner Alfred Vail who hit upon the three-part alphanumeric transmission code where combinations of long dash, short dot, and pause distinguished between different letters, numbers, and words (with more frequent letters like "e" using the shorter combinations like a single "dot").[8] Congress allocated money for Morse and his partners to build the first working intercity telegraph line between Washington, D.C., and Baltimore in the early 1840s, but then declined to take federal ownership of the nascent network. The telegraph soon saw significant military service in the Civil War, when even President Lincoln frequently used the system to communicate in code with field generals.[9] (Such wartime use also helped to bolster a tenuous telegraph industry and to train legions of linemen and operators on the intricacies of keeping the wired infrastructure working.) What followed was decades of build-out, experimentation, and consolidation in the telegraph industry, until this "Victorian Internet" became a fixture of rapid and distant

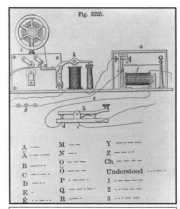

Wood engraving from Knight's American Mechanical Dictionary, *published in 1877, depicting the apparatus for sending and receiving coded telegraph messages, and the code itself, dots and dashes called "Morse Code" but actually invented by Alfrrd Vail.*

government and business communication, if still a luxury out of reach for most individual consumers.[10] And it demonstrated that the communication network was prone to different uses—and valued for different reasons—at the different scales of global communication (cable transmissions for commerce and diplomacy), national communication (coordinating intercity commerce and administration), and urban communication (wiring cities for automatic police, fire, and emergency signals).[11]

The coming of the telephone in the late-nineteenth century, and its gradual adoption for both local and long-distance personal and business communication in the early twentieth century, might today be considered a counterintuitive story of digital transmission technology (dots and dashes on the telegraph sounder) making way for analog transmission technology (speech on the telephone earpiece). But the telephone was much more than an improved telegraph; it enabled a fundamental shift in the very space and time of wired communication, moving the main node of messaging out of the corporate telegraph office and into the private business office or domestic home.[12] Highly visible local telegraph offices gave way to

A "photomechanical" print depicting the first instrument used in telegraphic transmission beween Baltimore and Washington in 1844. Alfred Vail (upper left) was at the Baltimore station.

Alexander Graham Bell (1847–1922) poses on the day of the inauguration of the long-distance telephone line from New York to Chicago, October 18, 1892.

more hidden local telephone exchanges; the national telegraph duopoly of Western Union and Postal Telegraph gave way to the national telephone monopoly of the Bell System; and ad-hoc telegram purchasers gave way to monthly telephone subscribers. As Rob MacDougall has shown, these transitions were accompanied by profound cultural concerns—and the marketing labor required to address them. For example, by building an advertising campaign that directly addressed the pulp-fiction fears of both new technology and monopoly capital as a menacing "spider" or "octopus" from about 1890 to 1910, "AT&T succeeded both in constructing a national telephone network and in selling that network as a model representation of the nation itself."[13]

For many decades, this new model of telephonic communication remained quite tied to the old notion of transportation. Claude Fisher has pointed out that when times were tough in the Great Depression, many rural households were careful to consider their connections to telephone networks and transportation networks in concert with each other, often abandoning their electrical communication subscription before letting go of their Model T.[14] This dynamic is still with us today: The processes of travel, transport, and communication remain intertwined, sometimes substituting for each other, but more often complementing and even encouraging each other. And it would be a mistake to assume that systems of telegraphy and telephony were used only as "point-to-point" communications technologies. Used rather in a one-to-many configuration, these technologies were instrumental in creating a new kind of national press that could collect information from far afield (commodity prices, official notices, and news reports) and then rapidly disseminate that information to a new national organization of participating newspapers through new membership organizations like the Associated Press. The Associated Press ushered in a new social and technological geography of news where "The timeliness of newspaper accounts declined in direct relation to distance from the center."[15]

A key development in the technology of the telephone was the Bell Company's new tactic of defining the economics within a technological network—renting the receivers directly to business and household users, achieving a monopoly on patents for the components of the network, and buying off any legal challengers with royalty-sharing agreements (as happened when Western Union agreed not to go into the telephone business in exchange for seventeen years' worth of telephone royalties from Bell). As MacDougall has pointed out, these communication strategies had widespread political significance, debated by local officials and consumers again and again in a struggle over the proper relationship between the local and the global in modern American society.[16] The Bell System's notion of "universal service" was at the center of this debate—wiring every household and business as both a utopian goal for bringing all consumers and citizens into political and economic contact, and a business strategy to claim "natural monopoly" status and to avoid onerous government regulation. The idea of universal service seemed to demonstrate that private capital could act in the public interest when it came to new communication media, a claim that continues to be reproduced in our current era of communication history.[17]

In the recording room of the New York Times in September 1942, an overseas shortwave radio-telephone operator receives and records messages from a correspondent in Berne, Switzerland. Telephone and telegraphic technologies were instrumental in creating a national press that could collect news from far away and rapidly disseminate that information.

But achieving a "natural monopoly" was anything but natural. The "system builders" who supposedly invented these infrastructures, tied in the public's mind to famous names such as Samuel Morse, Thomas Edison, and Alexander Graham Bell, gradually scaled up into complex, national corporate structures such as Western Union, Western Electric, and the Bell System, driven by publicly traded investments, professionally managed advertising, and university-educated engineers as much as the inspiration of genius.[18] In the process, these network firms battled each other over patent rights, labor relations, and territorial dominance for decades. Business historian Alfred Chandler has argued that these new electromechanical communication and transport infrastructures motivated corporate managers to reconceptualize their roles and exert a "visible hand" over production and distribution decisions that had previously been left to the market.[19]

This national growth and centralization, emblematic of the new networked industries of the late nineteenth century, reveals the contradictory position of the federal government with regard to regulation and competition in communication. On one hand, there were numerous moments when the federal government could have taken control of the wired communication industries of the telegraph and the telephone, especially under the administration of the post office, but declined

Syetem-builder Thomas Alva Edison strikes a thoughtful pose on October 16, 1905.

In October 1914, Lewis Hine photographed two telegraph messenger boys in Mobile, Alabama. Hine (1874–1940) was an American sociologist who regarded photography as a tool for social reform. The young lad is Emmet Brewster, age eleven.

to do so. This pattern of development contrasts with that of Great Britain, where the telegraph and telephone systems were from the start nationalized under the postal system. This American exceptionalism, some have argued, led to the competition required for innovation that kept U.S. telecommunications networks technologically ahead of those of the rest of the world.[20]

This anti-regulation argument is problematic, however. First of all, when the state refused to intervene in the telecommunications industry, the result was often not some sort of idealized competition, but instead monopoly concentration—first with Western Union and the telegraph in the late nineteenth century, and then with AT&T and the telephone in the early twentieth century. Second, the state did intervene quite aggressively in the wire services when it felt a national economic or military interest was at stake, as happened during both world wars. Third, the state actually subsidized both the telegraph and telephone systems heavily with its own use of the networks for military messaging, starting with the Civil War. So rather than lauding the "deregulation" that was supposed to have led to technological innovation in these industries, historians have begun to see how various regimes of regulation might have actually been preferred by the private owners of these telecommunications firms in order to allow them to avoid competition, plan technological obsolescence, or discipline labor.

Early in the twentieth century, a telegraph operator prints a telegram.

THE PLACE OF LABOR IN NETWORKED COMMUNICATION

Throughout this period of networked communication innovation and consolidation, neither the telegraph nor the telephone were simply systems of lightning lines and strategic management. Rather, these high-tech communication systems of the turn of the twentieth century always required the "high touch" of human hands, among them the outdoor linemen repairing downed wires after storms or vandalism, the indoor operators (both male and female) across a spatial division of labor in rural and urban telegraph and telephone offices, and the legions of uniformed child messengers who covered the "first mile" and "last mile" of both networks, transporting the ephemeral and virtual electronic impulses as very permanent and physical slips of glued yellow paper to those without a receiving device in their home or office. This vast labor force was absolutely necessary to the performance and profitability of the global telegraph network in particular; at the same time, it was

Helen Campbell, the first wireless operator for the National League for Women's Service, is seen here at work on May 8, 1917.

constantly subject to technological speedup, corporate paternalism, and other employee control measures by business managers seeking to avoid collective action by (and state scrutiny of) their workforce.[21]

This understanding that both the telegraph and telephone industries, for all their high technology, were actually incredibly labor intensive, has recently led historians to attempt to understand how firms repeatedly attempted to restructure their division of labor to maximize profits, and how laborers repeatedly attempted to organize their division of labor to improve working conditions. Amy Bix describes how the effort by the Bell System to install customer-dialed telephones dovetailed with the company's concern about an increasingly militant workforce of largely female telephone operators. For example, even though Bell added 32,000 operator jobs between 1920 and 1930, due to increased call volume, union members charged that this hiring involved mostly temporary, contingent positions. Over the same decade, Bell had replaced fully one-third of its telephones with new dial models, bypassing operators entirely.[22] And while African Americans had been excluded from much of the telecommunications industries through the early twentieth century, Venus Green has taken a first step at documenting the 1960s demographic transition from white to black among Bell System telephone operators, including the resulting strife tied to both a longstanding climate of racial prejudice among white coworkers and a reinvigorated attempt to enforce labor control by the largely white management.[23]

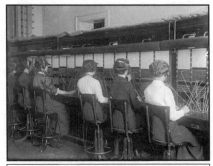

A "bank" of telephone operators at work during World War I.

Linemen at work near Newport News, Virginia, in March 1941, as photographed by John Vachon (1914–1975), who was well known for his unembellished scenes of working men and women. Although linemen such as these have become scarce, wireless networks still rely on a wired power grid.

A century and a half after they began, networked text and voice systems are still an important part of our communication infrastructure today; however, the meaning of point-to-point communication as an analytical category has been confounded by the ability of those points to shift over time and space. Rather than "land-line" or "fixed-point" telecommunications, today the telephone has gone mobile.[24] Such developments throw notions of the "network society" into disarray, as the network itself becomes not only more dynamic in space and time (phones moving about and switching on and off) but more fine-grained in spatial and temporal scale (tied to the daily movement of bodies rather than the long-term occupation of households and offices).[25]

But what we commonly refer to as "mobile" communication, because of its bodily portability, its use during daily commutes and business trips, and its ability to record one's movements throughout a data network, might just as well be understood under a different overriding concept. For example, calling mobile communication "wireless" communication instead would emphasize the different kind of physical capital investment needed to bring mobile networks to new regions. Wireless cell phone networks rely on fixed tranceivers and towers connected to a wired power grid. Such tranceivers often cluster in high-profit urban areas or follow the routes of interstate highways. Alternatively, reframing mobile communication as "personal" communication would emphasize the kinds of interactions through dense social networks that flow through these devices. In 2010, the latest cell phone handsets offered not only calling features but e-mail, text messaging, and social media functions from friend-monitoring services like Facebook to micro-blogging outlets like Twitter. And finally, reconsidering mobile communication as "ubiquitous" communication would emphasize not the availability of communication over space, but its presence and persistence over time. With your telephone always present on your body, you become always present to the telephone network. The previously distinct social situations of work time, recreation time, or family time collide together when one is constantly subject to interruption. In the end, perhaps "point-to-point communication" finally does become "universal service"—just not the way that the telephone company or its critics could have possibly forseen a century ago.

3

BROADCAST MASS COMMUNICATION: CREATING A CONSUMER CULTURE THROUGH FILM, RADIO, AND TELEVISION

Networked communication infrastructures increasingly linked individuals in the rapidly urbanizing and industrializing modern society of the early twentieth century—workers with managers, producers with consumers, voters with representatives. At the same time, another set of communication infrastructures were also being developed that cast message senders and message receivers into very different roles. These were the recorded and broadcast communication technologies of sound and vision—from wax-cylinder sound reproduction and silent cinema in the early 1900s to the national networks of radio and television broadcasters by the 1950s. Over time, these technologies ushered in a new commodification of information in rationalized multimedia packets, like the three-minute rock-'n-roll single or the ninety-minute VHS movie. They also tied the social processes of strategic communication, especially product marketing and political persuasion, more tightly to the advertising model of communication pioneered by the penny press, where media producers were willing to distribute their content practically for free in order to attract lucrative audiences of "eyeballs" for advertisers. And in these two political-economic transformations, the new broadcast communication infrastructure also spawned an entirely new academic pursuit: the study of message-making and its social effects.

RECORDED SOUND AND RECORDED VISION

The risks and rewards of broadcasting that captured the attention of the twentieth-century media theorists began in the nineteenth century with attempts to freeze sound and vision in some replayable and reproducible technological form. These experiments often flowed directly from the needs of what was then the current network communication infrastructure. Thomas Edison's recorded sound innovations came from his attempts to build new microphones and speakers for Western Union to challenge the Bell telephone patents. Thinking that recording voices might be a useful way for a telegraph company to use a telephone, Edison eventually developed and patented his first phonograph in 1878. But it was not until a decade later, in the late 1880s, that his laboratory improved the machine to target the market of office dictation and stenography. By the 1890s, competing firms targeted yet another market seeking more perfect phonograph perfor-

In an advertisement, c. 1897, a happy family enjoys its Edison Home Phonograph at Christmastime, with a portrait of Edison himself on the wall.

mance—using not just Edison's cylinders, but more easily reproducible wax discs—for the playing of recorded music in nickel arcades and parlor rooms.[1]

About the same time, experiments to capture visual motion were inaugurating a new science and practice of cinematography in both Europe and the United States. Edison's first commercial product, the Kinetoscope, produced short quarter-minute films that a viewer consumed individually at a stand-up kiosk. But soon movies could be projected onto a screen, and short one-minute features were introduced as a small part of longer vaudeville shows, intended for middle-class audiences paying 25¢ per show. By 1910 the most profitable venue for films had been transformed into the nickelodeon, with its 5¢ price more attractive to working-class immigrants and children watching the longer fifteen-minute narrative films as well as the newsreels.[2]

The construction of these new public commercial spaces meant that the early sound and film recording and playback systems represented not only a communication technology, but an urban spatial technology as well. This was a time when questions of order and disorder vexed social reformers, who often saw simplistic connections between working-class, immigrant communities in tenement districts and the sensational threats of vice, crime, and political revolution circulating in urban newspapers and dime novels.[3] The new sites for recorded media consumption—dark and crowded venues filled with wondrous images especially designed to attract children and youth—seemed to threaten more traditional and supposedly uplifting forms of cultural recreation, like libraries, parks, playgrounds, and church outings.[4]

But audiences flocked to experience these new media, and within a few short decades a vibrant global industry in recorded entertainment had blossomed. Movie studios and theater owners searched for new markets, greater economies of scale, and tighter forms of economic control over the production and distribution of entertainment. The combination of sound with film that finally arrived at the tail-end of the 1920s was a technological convergence long sought after by the motion picture industry, but not necessarily because executives thought audiences were clamoring for this new mode of storytelling. Silent movies had long been accompanied by "live" sound, from orchestral music to sound "effects" to narrated speech. Prerecording all of this sound and automatically delivering it in synchronization with a filmed presentation would return control over the performance (both the auditory experience and the expense of the orchestra) back to the studios and to those theater owners who could afford to become wired for sound. These "talkies" motivated the need for another round of technological innovation, as the overseas market for Hollywood films now found it necessary either to subtitle or revoice (dub) these talking films.[5]

Dressed up for a Sunday movie mantinee in the spring of 1941. The photographer was Russell Lee.

The rest of the century would bring a continuous series of technological refinements to the audio/visual recording and duplicating process, especially a shift from physical and chemical traces (grooves in wax and silver on film) to electromagnetic and digital signals (waveforms on videotape and bits on audio CDs). But the intertwined history of sound and vision recording, playback, duplication, and distribution should be understood less as a series of technological advances in reproducing the experience of hearing a live performance, and more as the development of an entire system for commodifying the product of, restructuring the labor of, reorganizing the spaces of, and redefining the meaning of the live performance. Movie theaters and music halls were forced to adapt architecturally to each new technology of sound, as Emily Thompson has recently shown, with new acoustical engineers concerned as much with keeping sound out of certain spaces as with maximizing sound's impact in others.[6] Professional musicians who had spent the last decades of the nineteenth century organizing national unions found their industry losing tens of thousands of jobs in the early decades of the twentieth century.[7] And consumers too participated in each of these rounds of sociotechnical change, adopting what Jonathan Sterne has called "audile techniques"—both new ways of listening and new ways of understanding what one is listening to—built out of previous experiences with auditory technologies as diverse as stethoscopes and telegraph sounders.[8] All of this social adjustment points to the creation of what David Morton called a new "recording culture," at the boundaries between a commercial, business technology and a cultural, aesthetic technology.[9]

RADIO AND TELEVISION

The radio and television broadcasting industries would eventually connect to these infrastructures of sound and vision recording. But the origins of these twentieth-century transmission infrastructures were, again, tied to the networked communication tools of the nineteenth century. First conceptualized as "wireless telegraphy," the idea of sending radio transmissions from a broadcast center to an audience periphery—rather than from a single transmission site to a single reception site, like the telegraph—grew out of a 1910s and 1920s hobbyist culture.

Listening to the radio. Photo by Under-wood & Underwood, 1909.

Susan Douglas described the first wave of amateur boy radio enthusiasts as "primarily young, white, middle-class boys and men who built their own stations in their bedrooms, attics, or garages," and whose exploits were quickly romanticized in the dime novels sold to that very same demographic. She later characterized this urban hobbyist culture of early radio as akin to "the spread of home computing in the late 1980s and 1990s."[10]

By the mid-1920s, broadcast radio had quickly moved from a hobbyist culture to a commercial marketplace. But even before the NBC and CBS radio networks were established in 1926–27, educational institutions had established more than a hundred stations as a public service. Although the Radio Act of 1927 specifically acknowledged this important precedent by encouraging the new Federal Radio Commission to favor stations that acted in the "public interest, convenience, or necessity," by the mid-1930s the commercial network stations accounted for 97 percent of all nighttime broadcasting, when the listening audience was greatest.[11]

This "network model" of broadcasting had two components. On one hand, it represented a "technological fix": a way of inventing and orienting a technological infrastructure to achieve some social, political, or economic goal. In this case, the goal was to accurately and efficiently transmit a single centralized radio signal out to millions of individual household radio receivers across a continent. The broadcasters leased existing long-distance telephone land lines to send programs across a national landscape before beaming them wirelessly to local receivers. On the other hand, the network model also represented what we might call a "spatial fix": a way of reorganizing human activity across space and time for some particular purpose. In this case, the network model was an innovative way for the economic patent-owning partnership of AT&T and RCA to reap economies of scale in both centralized radio production and national radio advertising.

But supporting radio through the technological and spatial fixes of network production and national advertising was neither the only solution possible, nor the most obvious solution at the time. In the early 1920s, then-Secretary of Commerce Herbert Hoover claimed it was "inconceivable that we should allow so great a possibility for service and for news and for entertainment and education, for vital commercial purposes to be drowned in advertising chatter."[12] The notion of advertiser-supported radio broadcasting was "condemned as a crass invasion of people's private lives," according to Douglas, and developing the commercialized system we have today was "a contested process, with educators and labor organizers, corporate interests, amateur operators, and the government all advancing their very different visions for the future."[13] Although previous mass media like newspapers and magazines had been supported by advertising for nearly a century, the intrusion of commercial messages (and, increasingly, political messages) upon music, drama, comedy, or news broadcasts vividly brought the private control of media to the attention of activists.[14] Advocates of the networked advertising model, however, pointed to the skyrocketing sales of products like Pepsodent toothpaste in the wake of its sponsorship of the controversial but nevertheless popular *Amos 'n' Andy* radio comedy/drama in 1928.[15]

In March 1942, a Washington, D.C., class listens to a radio broadcast about South America. Public-interest broadcasting such as this was a special emphasis in the Radio Act of 1927.

Over time, advertising, entertainment, and public service on the radio settled into a temporal "flow," a constant stream of programming in drama, comedy, music, and news sponsored by commercial concerns and appearing at regular intervals throughout the day and week.[16] The temporal patterns of sound broadcasting on the radio soon provided a template for the temporal patterns of visual broadcasting on television when this technology, in the works since the 1930s, finally emerged into the postwar American consumer economy.[17] Grown out of the technological advances in the production of vacuum tubes and cathode-ray tubes linked to radio and radar systems in World War II, the first black-and-white television widely available to consumers in the postwar era was affordable to middle-class households for about $375.[18] By the time color television was introduced in 1954, the industry was well into its "Golden Age" as measured by the sheer rate of household adoption, media attention, and program innovation.

Not all entrants to this new market were successful. Allen DuMont had been making television cathode-ray tubes for over a decade before his small broadcast network

Freeman Gosden and Charles Correll perform as Amos 'n' Andy *in the NBC radio studios. This popular (but later controversial) program brought skyrocketing sales to products such as Pepsodent toothpaste. NBC Photograph, 1935.*

Thanksgiving and football on the cover of The New Yorker, November 26, 1949. Art by Constantin Alajalov.

went on the air in 1946, full of cash from wartime engineering contracts. The DuMont network broadcast for barely a decade, never acquiring the kind of allied radio network infrastructure that each of the "big three" television broadcasters had at their disposal.[19] But not all successes grew from a national network model, either. In the early 1950s, the FCC reserved some 242 channels across the nation for community-based, noncommercial and educational television stations, 76 of which went online slowly but steadily between 1956 and 1962.[20] These stations set the stage for the Carnegie Commission report on television in 1967, which laid the groundwork for the later Public Broadcasting System by arguing "a well-financed and well-directed educational television system, substantially larger and far more pervasive and effective than that which now exists in the United States, must be brought into being if the full needs of the American public are to be served."[21]

On the whole, though, the rapid, widespread, and intensive adoption of television by so many U.S. households in the 1950s ushered in a sort of media monoculture. As historian James Baughman described, "Americans who had once spent their evenings using a variety of mass media—films, newspapers, periodicals, and radio—were likely by the mid and late 1950s to watch television." In an extended example of the historical changes that followed from the rapid adoption of broadcast television in the 1950s, Baughman illustrated how previ-

Television studio at Capitol Radio Engineering Institute. Photograph by Theodor Horydczak, c. 1945.

ous forms of communication, from entertainment in radio and film to journalism in newspapers and magazines, all attempted to adapt to a new media ecology in which the space of the American living room was now directly connected to entertainment firms, news organizations, and product advertisers. Television drew on the visual immediacy (and legacy content) of cinema, organized itself into the dramatic, comedy, and game-show programming genres of radio, provided a daily news update to rival the newspaper, and brought to the nation the vivid global imagery of *Life* magazine. In response, radio station owners diversified into channel-based music genres, newspaper owners increasingly targeted new suburban audiences with new lifestyle features, and filmmakers pushed the boundaries of cinema outside of the accepted norms of the living room with sex, violence, and high art. Only the glossy general-interest magazines withered, not for lack of circulation, but for lack of competitive "cost per thousand" advertising rates when compared to prime-time television marketing media buys.[22]

The geography of television viewing was key here. Even more so than radio, television was wrapped into other postwar ideals of suburbanization, consumerism, and gender roles within the nuclear family. As Lynn Spigel notes, "Television was supposed to bring the family together but still allow for social and sexual divisions in the home."[23] Video consoles began to displace the piano or the fireplace hearth in the ideal middle-class home, presenting round-the-clock idealized images of suburban family life in both programming and advertising. And as commercials on the radio (and later television) were coordinated with campaigns in print, at the point of sale, and even in the outdoor environment, the technology of broadcast media intersected with the technology of suburban housing development and rapid automobile transport, not only in the more intensive development of billboard advertising, but in the siting and design of strip-mall architecture itself.[24]

REMAKING THE AUDIENCE

Central to the twentieth century's infrastructure of recorded and broadcast sound and vision was the increasingly important social category of the "audience." Audiences for public speeches and dramatic performances had long been part of politics and the theater, but they were always bounded by the time and space of a performance. Elite concerns over audiences focused on what individuals might bring to the site of the performance, according to Richard Butsch: "the degenerate or unruly people who came to the theater, and what they might do, once gathered."[25]

By the early twentieth century, technologies for bridging time and space began to change this. For example, in the years between the dominance of the print media and the rise of broadcast media, from about 1904 to 1932, the transporta-

John Philip Sousa leading his band at a Chautauqua, ca. 1925.

William Jennings Bryan, three-time Democratic presidential candidate, addresses a Madison, Indiana, Chautauqua on July 6, 1901.

tion network of the Chautauqua circuit—a diverse and ever-changing set of rural road-shows comprising educators, entertainers, and evangelists intended to serve the needs of adult education and uplift—brought ideas, music, and drama to big tents in small towns. These events helped build the political celebrity of William Jennings Bryan and Robert La Follette alongside the entertainment celebrity of ventriloquist Edgar Bergen.[26] At the same time, new urban spaces for the nickel cinema, building on the old vaudeville tradition, promised to bring perfectly reproduced images to all viewers regardless of location, just as the radio brought perfectly reproduced sounds to all households who could afford a set. Historian Deborah Brant has pointed out how such media messages worked in tandem with past traditions of literacy: children might write and perform their own skits for family and friends based on popular films, or write letters to radio personalities in search of prizes and autographs.[27] But Butsch points out that such changing practices of literacy, consumption, and civic participation also led to social fears, where "worries focused on the dangers of reception, how media messages might degenerate audiences," especially children.[28]

These early ideas of the mass audience often carried with them notions of technological determinism. Especially in the wake of the propaganda campaigns of World War I—the origin of the iconic "Uncle Sam" poster campaign—the means of mass communication were thought to act as a "hypodermic needle" or a "magic bullet," injecting ideas into a passive, undifferentiated, readily manipulated crowd. Such a view motivated both the dreams of new public relations experts and the fears of their detractors, as institutional communicators not only attempted to sell products and ideas to the public, but also came to believe that theirs was a necessary function of discipline and control in a technological mass society. The connections between audience as "crowd" and working class as "mob" were not hard to find. Both on the factory floor and in the clerical office, advocates of "Scientific Management" techniques like Frederick Winslow Taylor, William Henry Leffingwell, and Frank Gilbreth argued that only through

United States Navy recruiting poster, 1941.

the expert study of work processes, the rational decomposition of those processes into their key components, and the scientific reconstruction of those processes in the most time-efficient and cost-effective way possible, could businesses succeed in both controlling their labor forces and outproducing their competitors. Such practices mobilized all of the information technologies of their times, especially still and motion cameras, to minutely record, time, and analyze worker motions in order to extract the greatest amount of labor with the least amount of idle "waste" from office secretaries and assembly-line workers alike.[29]

Frederick Winslow Taylor (1856–1915), "Father of Scentific Management." This pen-and-ink drawing by Robert Kastor is autographed on December 5, 1913, with the inscription, "A big day's work of a big day's pay."

These early industrial engineers, attempting to control the manufacture of products and services within the large bureaucratic corporation, shared much with those attempting to define (and defend) the "manufacture of consent" in the public sphere, such as Walter Lippmann and Edward Bernays.[30] Lippmann in particular—with experience as an academic, a muckraking magazine reporter, a New York newspaper editor, and a propagandist with the Inter-Allied Propaganda Commission in World War I—exemplified the dilemma in the conclusion to his 1922 *Public Opinion* when he spoke of the challenge of "using the method of reason to deal with an unreasoning world." Given the rampant "stereotypes" held by everyday members of the media audience—"the stored up images, the preconceptions, and prejudices"—Lippmann was dismayed to conclude that "public opinions must be organized for the press if they are to be sound, not by the press as is the case today."[31] Bernays, a fellow wartime communicator with Lippmann who was schooled in the theories of the basic irrationality of the human psyche as put forth by his own uncle Sigmund Freud, took these ideas one step further. In his 1928 book *Propaganda*, he argued that it was good and proper that a certain class of communicators exercise "natural leadership," given "their ability to supply needed ideas and by their key positions in the social structure."[32] Thus the profession of public relations was born.

Walter Lippmann (1889–1974) was a Pulitzer Pize-winning syndicated columnist who introduced the expression "Cold War" to his readers and for many years published his analyses of the relationship of persuasion, propaganda, and public opinion.

Later conceptions of the audience shifted the other way, understanding readers, listeners, and viewers to be highly individualized and differentiated, responding to media messages under more "limited effects" conditions, and always acting to serve their own well-understood "uses and gratifications." Much of this understanding came from the academic research performed by political scientists-turned-communication-researchers in the study of election messages in broadcast media.[33] Such theories correctly challenged the totalizing persuasion notions of the past, but ran the risk of assuming too much consumer choice in a realm where, historically, fewer and fewer larger and larger media firms have exerted targeted control over more and more of the information and entertainment content from which audiences try to choose.[34]

But despite the changing trends in the new academic field of communication studies, industry-based research into defining and understanding the audience has been key to the deployment of these new mass media technologies from the start.[35] As early as 1903, Chicago advertising firm J. Walter Thompson became one of the first to systematically perform market research, correlating consumer demographics to the way they reacted to various brands and advertisements. But careful, rational research, especially when later combined with new Freudian theories of the mind and personality, did not necessarily lead to careful, rational pitches for products. According to cultural historian Jackson Lears, "The more childlike or irrational the consumer's image became, the more justifiable seemed the resort to carnivalesque sensationalism or emotional appeals."[36] By the late 1970s, as the children of the postwar baby boom reached adulthood in force, marketing to a broad middle class was waning and "articles and advertisements in the trade press depicted the upper-middle and upper classes as multifaceted and continually open to new experiences," or "differentiated by lifestyle," with internal slogans like the one *Time* magazine used in the mid-1980s: "More than ever, real consumers are concentrated at the top."[37]

In February 1943 documentary photographer Ann Rosener took this photo of Ruth Anderson, a San Francisco radio news reporter, reading to her audience from a teletype.

Today the audience is increasingly understood, within the largely advertising-supported sociotechnical system of electronic broadcasting, as a labor product—or even a labor force itself. As Oscar Gandy put it, "Commercial broadcasters 'produce audiences' or, more precisely, blocks of time during which it is possible to communicate with audiences, which they then sell to advertisers."[38] Media theorist Dallas Smythe took this idea one step farther by conceptualizing the labor that audiences perform on the part of the broadcasters as what produces value, or profit, for network owners.[39] Such labor is even subject to social and technological speed-up, not unlike that of a Taylorist factory floor, when commercial frequency and presence increases throughout daily life such that "audiences are made to work harder by having to view more individual commercials for each minute of entertainment."[40]

REGULATING BROADCAST MEDIA

One constant in the history of changing concerns about the broadcast media's power over the audience was the appeal for some sort of government regulation over private media owners and operators. Historian Douglas Craig has called the early regulatory response to radio broadcasting a combination of exceptionalism and utopianism to highlight the fact that many state and industry officials saw radio as qualitatively different from other forms of mass media, especially newspapers. Radio seemed to have such a broad reach and diversity in terms of its potential audience that harnessing it for the public interest, rather than solely for private profit, was of utmost concern. Thus the utopian hope for radio as a medium of political and cultural education masked a dystopian fear of radio as an all-powerful mechanism for commercial and political propaganda.[41] As William Boddy has pointed out, licensing this mechanism to private capital posed a contradiction: "that the federal license confers a privilege, not a right, to the broadcaster to operate in 'the public interest' using public airwaves, and that the license establishes and protects the broad de facto property rights of private operators of television and radio stations under restricted oversight of network operations and program content."[42]

Historians of the interplay between state and market forces in the deployment of these communication systems have shown how regulatory decisions and competitive strategies are never solely pinned either to technological constraints or to social norms, but must negotiate the interaction of both. For example, take the case of state regulation over the broadcast spectrum—that relatively small range of electromagnetic frequencies over which individual radio signals (and later television signals) might feasibly be broadcast. The "scarcity" of the spectrum comes not only from its absolute limits in size, but from the fact that pumping more power through a signal can cause interference with neighboring signals on the spectrum, especially in the same local area. Thus the actual availability of the broadcast spectrum in time and space—especially when pinned to a national network geography of dense urban centers with many competing channels and remote rural areas desperate for broadcast attention—depended on the expert claims of electrical engineers regarding questions of signal strength, channel overlap, and reception quality. But at the same time, "non-technocratic" questions of serving the public interest through private broadcasting, or even of ascertaining who, in a given local broadcast market, the "public" really was and what serving their best interests meant, carried great weight with regulatory groups like the Federal Communications Commission (FCC).[43]

The development, and later difficulties, of the sociotechnical system of public television in the United States provides a good example here. Disparaging commercial television as a "vast wasteland," Congress enthusiastically created a Corporation for Public Broadcasting in the late 1960s, meant to bring quality and education back to the airwaves. Yet only a few years later, President Richard Nixon's conservative administration was denouncing the new Public Broadcasting System (PBS) as a haven for so-called "liberal elite bias"—defined at that time as a bias against the idea that what was best for corporate business interests was best for America—a charge that continued to be recycled for the next three decades and counting, even as PBS itself increasingly relied upon the underwriting of major oil and agribusiness corporations in order to sustain its revenue stream in the face of state budget cuts.[44]

Cable television was another technological fix for television transmission that was soon reimagined as a social fix for television regulation. Originally thought of as "community antenna television" (CATV) to allow for the retransmission of broadcast signals over rugged terrain in Pennsylvania, to many in the late 1960s cable offered a way to both bring "electronic education" to community colleges through closed-circuit instructional channels and to "wire the cities" to defuse the racial, generational, and economic strife of the new urban protests and riots.[45] Yet within a decade the coaxial connection to television was known less for "public, educational, and government" (PEG) programming, and more as a window on the edgy teen and adult fare of MTV and HBO, once again making profitable peace between television and the older mass communication systems of radio and film.[46]

Even the technology of the magnetic videotape, originally envisioned as a democratic means of media production to be disseminated to news studios, vocational schools, and cable-access television cooperatives nationwide, found itself taking on a commodity form as gas stations, convenience marts, mom-and-pop shops, and even public libraries introduced the concept of "renting a movie" to a generation of TV-watchers in the 1980s.[47] And while the television industry itself benefited from the convenience and efficiency of videotape production, these improvements accompanied the wholesale turnover of local television news from federally mandated "loss leader" (something stations produced for their publics only to keep their FCC license) into a highly marketed profit center with the new "Eyewitness News" format pioneered by Detroit news director Al Primo.[48] Whether the technologically improved world of TV was still a "wasteland" by the 1990s might have been debatable, but TV was certainly not anti-corporate.

MINORITY MEDIA PRODUCTION AND CONSUMPTION

Even when it had room to act, media regulation in the "public interest" was faced with the thorny question of just who the public was. A certain degree of age, gender, and ethnic diversity was present within the broadcast industries from the start; for example, although their opportunities for advancement may have been severely limited, women participated in both radio and television production, especially during times of more fluid and changing gender roles in the workplace, such as during World War II.[49] But early broadcast economics, funded by national advertising campaigns, often constructed mainstream radio and television audiences with a "least common denominator" strategy that eliminated difference and conflict from programming. As a result, diverse communities of all sorts—cast in terms of race, ethnicity, language, class, culture, age, or gender—were often forced to program for themselves.

Such minority-driven programming was often structured by geography, especially in the early years of broadcasting before strict licensing regulation and network consolidation, when small stations in remote areas could serve local audiences with targeted entertainment and advertising that would have been shut out of the larger broadcast markets. In some of these social niches, such as that of conservative Protestant religious programming, there was plenty of revenue to be made apart from the mainstream.[50] At the same time, however, cultural traditions of music and performance from minority communities, from jazz and blues to rock and roll, were increasingly appropriated for broadcast to mainstream audiences in search of novel content. Over time, the competitive economics of broadcast communication and the increase in channels for programming slowly shifted, first to accommodate and then to target minority audiences of all sorts. Recent work focusing on African Americans in sound recording, for example, shows radio at work in both the integration of these communities to the cultural mainstream and in the public challenges that would culminate in the civil rights movement.[51]

For many minority communities, the story of mass media throughout the twentieth century centered around the tension between a communication system that would serve the public interest without regard to profit, versus one that would profitably provide what the public was interested in. Nowhere was this tension more evident than in the decades-long effort to bring text to television for deaf and hard-of-hearing viewers through closed captioning. Although the technological fix for TV captioning was developed in the early 1970s—through both the non-profit activist efforts of deaf educators and state-subsidized research at the National Bureau of Standards and PBS—it took another two

Rufus P. Turner, a student at the Armstrong Technical High School in Washington, D.C., operates a station broadcasting sermons and choir music from St. Augustine's Roman Catholic Church, January 12, 1926.

decades of trying various voluntary "public-private partnerships" between the federal government and the private broadcasting industry before the necessary regulations were passed to demand that practically all programs, on all channels, at all times of day, deserved captioning. These debates were not simply a question of minority accessibility to the media, however; the communication technology of captioning was recast as a tool of literacy education, a way to Americanize immigrants, and a crucial convenience for hearing audiences consuming television out in public, away from the stereotypical single-family home. Only after the technological system for connecting text to television was normalized through all areas of the television production, distribution, and consumption chain, could media corporations realize that such multi-modal indexing of information was of key importance as the legacy content of nearly half a century of television became digitized, commodified, and repurposed for just-in-time Internet delivery.[52]

The efforts of broadcast audiences outside of the mainstream to assert their worth in the face of a sociotechnical media system that persistently denies them any value illustrates well that, just as the richest explanations of technology in society are rooted in both a careful assembly of historical context and a wide-ranging development of social theory, so the richest explanations of communication behavior see audiences neither as wholly passive nor wholly active, but as historical actors both constrained and enabled by the informational infrastructures within which they live.

4

COMPUTER-MEDIATED COMMUNICATION: DIGITAL CONVERGENCE IN A NEW ECONOMY

The broadcast communication institutions and infrastructures seemed to culminate at mid-century with the rise of the mass television audience as a shared point of focus for entertainment, advertising, education, and political participation projects of all sorts. Yet these technologies paradoxically carried hopes for individualization, interactivity, and interpenetration with other media, from the recurring efforts to market a workable "picturephone" to the growing dream of the wired city through interactive cable television.[1] This story of communication technology from mid-century onward was one in which new convergences between communication, commerce, and culture were increasingly mediated by a technology not originally conceptualized as one of communication, but of calculation: the general-purpose, programmable digital computer. Here, we briefly consider the way historians have explored this computer-enabled digital convergence of media technologies, institutions, and practices in the late twentieth century.

DEVELOPING THE DIGITAL COMPUTER

At the end of the first half-century of digital computing, historians have published the first comprehensive narratives on the development of computing hardware and software—both of which proceeded through the intertwined logics and projects of the postwar military-industrial-academic complex.[2] On the surface, it might seem to be a story of "Moore's Law" and technological determinism—the notion that, simply because of the natural qualities of silicon and electrons, coupled with the obvious market imperative to push these qualities to their limits, computer processing power will continue to increase in speed and capacity while decreasing in size and cost in predictable leaps every eighteen months or so. We like to point out how the large, expensive, power-hungry "glass house" mainframe computers of the 1950s slowly shrank in size, through the refrigerator-sized "minicomputers" of the 1960s and 1970s, finally reaching the desktop and the laptop in the form of the "personal computer" of the 1980s and 1990s. But this is also a story of system-building and brand-building, with early firms like IBM and later ones like Microsoft building market share

The Univac I system. In the foreground is the back of a console with cover removed to show components. To the right is a row of tape drives. Image courtesy of Computer History Museum.

through technological standardization and the targeting of specific computing communities with different products, from business data processing to scientific computing.

As Paul Edwards has pointed out, whether they are focused on technologies or on institutions, our histories of computing have often been limited to either what he calls the "machine logic" story, prioritizing the development of symbolic systems and programming languages for machine computation, or the "machine calculation" story, foregrounding the engineering firms marketing computers to the corporate world, and the economic gains these machines were claimed to have ushered in.[3] Narratives of genius and innovation dominate our first pass through this business history of computing hardware and software; stories abound of Eckert and Mauchly creating the ENIAC at the University of Pennsylvania, or William Shockley developing a new solid-state amplifier called the "transistor" at Bell Labs in 1947. Both of these computational innovations were based on the desire to scale up or speed up previous manual or electromechanical technologies. In the case of the ENIAC, a general-purpose programmable, digital computer based on vacuum tubes was meant to replace legions of female "computers" employed to perform wartime ballistic calculations (even though many of these mathematical workers went on to, in effect, become the first programmers of the ENIAC itself).[4] Similarly, the transistor's advantage over the vacuum tube for digital circuits was not only its smaller size and lower energy consumption,

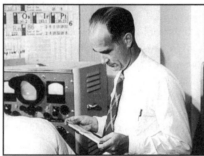

At Bell Labs in 1947, William Shockley (1910–89) devised a solid-state amplifier that was dubbed a "transistor." AIP Emilio Segrè Visual Archives, Brattain Collection.

but also its ease of mass production and longer-term reliability, again helping to reduce the overall human labor costs of computation.[5]

Computing development in the United States is especially subject to a dramatic retelling where producers and users alike seem to be acting through pure market rationality; computers are supposedly promoted and adopted only where they "make sense" for increasing output and reducing costs in business, government, and scientific operations (or, to put it another way, only when historical actors develop an adequate "learning base" to make efficient use of these new computational tools).[6] In this way, corporate managers have moved beyond their "visible hand" strategies of using networked communication and transportation technologies, developed at the turn of the twentieth century, to a similar sort of "digital hand" strategy of managing the risks of capitalism through computerization at the end of the century.[7] But the guidance of the "digital hand" is not as straightforward as these histories would suggest. Shockley's own spinoff, start-up firm to market solid-state electronics, Shockley Semiconductor Laboratory, was an economic failure (though it did serve to incubate a second round of spinoff firms that went on to great success in the integrated circuit market). The early computing industry, especially as embodied by IBM, took many of its cues (for better and for worse) from a previous round of electromechanical punch-card tabulating machines—and abandoning this profitable business for the risk of unproven digital calculating systems was not an easy or obvious step for either vendors or customers.[8] And JoAnne Yates has demonstrated the contingent nature of consumer adoption of computers in her study of how the life insurance industry, seemingly a natural fit for technological calculation, was affected by many so-called "structuring factors" such as professional associations, government regulation, and a fluctuating market in its transition to computer technology.[9]

Histories that focus on the military and scientific development of computer technology have taken a different path. Here, rather than market rationality, defense rationalization has been cited for computer system-building.[10] ENIAC's application to ballistics calculations in World War II is only the first example of this story. Another well-known example is the "Semi-Automatic Ground Environment" project, SAGE, designed as the first air-defense system with a digital computer at its center.[11] With government contracts to commercial organizations booming during the Cold War, communications and electronics firms of all sorts—IBM, General Electric, Bell Telephone, Sperry Rand, Raytheon, and RCA, to name a few—received over half of their funding from the federal government through the 1950s as they worked to develop computing fixes to defense-related problems. These technologies were, ideally, spun off into the commercial sector. For example, the SAGE system relied on digital communications over telephone lines to relay data from radar installations to the computer center, an architecture that would see commercial application in the first online airline reservation system, SABRE.[12]

In 1942, female workers as far as the eye can see in the Priorities Division of the War Production Board. The ENIAC was designed to replace such "manual" labor.

Paul Edwards has analyzed this period through what he calls a discourse of the "closed world"—the way that the very foundational notions of cybernetics, remote sensing, and artificial-intelligence research became intimately tied to the utopian promise of computerizing the "Command, Control, Communications, and Intelligence" functions of a globally extended defense force. With the closed world of computer models and simulations of military risks and responses, technological development became self-perpetuating.[13]

FROM REPLACING HUMAN LABOR TO AUGMENTING HUMAN LABOR

Just as a redefinition of the audience was the thread that connected decades of broadcast communication history, a redefinition of the worker sits at the heart of the history of digital convergence. From the early days of mainframe computing, computer scientists and management entrepreneurs pondered whether to harness these calculation engines for the automation of human labor out of the workplace, or for the augmentation of human action within the workplace. On the demand side, many of the first customers of the nascent computer industry were seeking labor efficiencies not only by introducing calculating and data processing technology, but also by reorganizing their business processes through "systems analysis" to remove redundancies, restructure wage and skill requirements, and reap new efficiencies over time and space. The underlying goal was to eliminate low-wage labor through automation, and countless theories of the "postindustrial society" grew from this dream.[14] Yet the paradox of introducing information technology into the workplace is that new forms of skill and labor are then required.[15] As a result, systems analysts turned to using technology to augment the work of a new class of "information professionals" as a second route to increased productivity. Thus while some teams of computer scientists attempted to build a new science of artificial intelligence with the hopes of passing the "Turing Test" and creating a system that could replace human decision-making, others like Douglas Engelbart's group at Stanford Research Institute pioneered such tools as graphic user interfaces, the computer mouse, and teleconferencing to create a computer system able to interact in real time with a new kind of "knowledge worker."[16]

Employees of the U.S. Bureau of the Census operating mechanical sorters for the classification and distribution of punch cards, c.1939.

However, these questions of computing and labor actually have much earlier roots. After all, as historian David Alan Grier has shown, the term "computer" itself was drawn from the human occupation of manual calculation using the new technological developments such as slide rules, adding machines, and punch-card tabulators in the late nineteenth and early twentieth centuries.[17] Similarly, the question of the proper relationship between human and machine had been simmering for decades during the "second industrial revolution" fueled by electricity and oil, coming to a boiling point in the Great Depression (with fears that an over-mechanized society was at least partially to blame for widespread industrial unem-

Transferring information on punch-card machines at the U.S. Bureau of the Census, c. 1939.

ployment). For example, Elizabeth F. Baker's *Displacement of Men by Machines*, published in 1933, explored the way that new optical/electrical typesetting machines had made whole professions within the commercial printing industry obsolete within a matter of decades.[18] And as historian David Mindell has shown, it was telephone engineers attempting to conquer long-distance efficiency problems of the Bell network, military engineers attempting to streamline the interaction of pilots and their weapons systems, and electrical engineers attempting to use analog "differential analyzers" to level loads on long-distance power lines, who pushed forward ideas about feedback and control in human/machine systems (something called "cybernetics") long before the first digital computer.[19]

NETWORKING AND PERSONALIZING THE COMPUTER

This question of creating an infrastructure for the augmentation of human work was at the heart of the computer's convergence with communication. The computer first became a communication tool with the development of networking protocols, connections, and interfaces that allowed different pieces of hardware to exchange data with each other. But for the most important computer networking project of mid-century, the Defense Department's ARPANET, simple communication between computer sites was not the main goal. Instead, ARPANET was created with computation in mind: in an era of largely custom-built mainframe computers controlled by university laboratories and defense contractors, each with its own unique computational strengths and tools, a national network was seen as a way for researchers to efficiently utilize each others' hardware and software at a distance, for their own purposes. Some of the ARPANET innovations, like the use of a new distributed, decentralized "packet switching" communications protocol (where messages were split into bite-sized bits and routed around the network asynchronously) rather than the more common "circuit switching" method (where a single open channel from sender to receiver needed to be maintained for the duration of the message transmission) had their origins in military values of

The term "computer" was drawn from the work of manual calculation using new technological devices such as the adding machine.

"survivability, flexibility, and high performance." Other innovations, however, such as the creation of a "layered" communication system where computers first translated their messages into a new, common protocol before exchanging them, were meant to overcome questions of labor in the construction and maintenance of the network.

Each host site would be responsible for creating and maintaining its own "interface message processor" tied to its specific hardware and software. A central group might create communication standards, but a decentralized division of labor grew up to enact these standards in practice. And the ARPANET innovations most associated with today's communication practices—time-sharing, electronic mail, bulletin board services—grew up out of a third logic, a more open and cooperative set of labors initiated and managed by the collective of students, faculty, and professionals let loose as "users" on the network through their institutional affiliations. Far from simply a technological fix, then, the ARPANET, and the Internet into which it evolved, must be understood as a set of social innovations as well, between military, corporate, and academic actors.[20]

In the 1970s, shortly after the introduction of the ARPANET, personal computing emerged both because of a new communication infrastructure technology—the microprocessor developed by Intel—and the unsatisfied demand for a new scale of computing experience that could be served neither by the corporate mainframe computer nor what were then known as less expensive "mini" computers. At a time when such refrigerator-sized minicomputers cost around $20,000, and buying computer "cycles" on a mainframe time-sharing system cost between $10 and $20 per hour, personal computers were hobbyist creations, culminating in the $400 Altair 8800 kit in 1975. Much like the early cable television systems that inspired activists in the late 1960s, these new machines were lauded by counterculture

Microprocessor developed by Intel. Image courtesy of Computer History Museum.

icons like Stewart Brand (of the *Whole Earth Catalog*) and "computer liberation" enthusiasts such as Ted Nelson (who self-published a do-it-yourself primer on computer programming in 1974 called *Computer Lib*).[21] Nelson's claim for such new technology—still echoed by the advertising campaigns of PC makers decades later—was that "People have legitimate complaints about the way computers are used, and legitimate ideas for ways they should be used, which should no longer be shunted aside."[22] But like the radio enthusiasts of a half-century earlier, the largely young and male computer hobbyists inspired by the likes of Brand and Nelson helped usher in what eventually became a global, ubiquitous, and very corporate communication infrastructure.

In the home, however, computing was always more about content than calculation. Grown directly from experiments in the military-industrial-academic world of the ARPANET, the mass-communication medium of video games emerged as a major consumer electronics industry in the late 1970s. First appearing, much like the nickelodeons of the early century, in restaurants and taverns, video games with themes drawn from professional television sports, science-fiction cinema, or Japanese comic-book culture soon entered the middle-class home through vendors like Atari, Magnavox, Mattel, and later Nintendo. The industry crashed and was revived repeatedly through the 1980s, with major media companies like Sony and Microsoft finally entering the field in the 1990s. Just as with the media fears of the earlier part of the century, computer gaming was often assigned "magic bullet" status, feared to have the power both to educate the children of tomorrow without need of human intervention, and to corrupt those same children into efficient, cold-blooded killers.[23]

But there was one aspect of the computer, both in the home and in the office, that irrevocably distinguished it from the broadcast media from which it drew so much cultural inspiration. Just as the meaning of mainframe computation began to shift with the networked interconnections of the ARPANET (transforming over the 1980s and 1990s into the Internet), the economic utility and the social meaning of personal computing changed when those computers (and the persons using them) became connected through digital communication networks of their own. If the Internet represented the key sociotechnical system for "wide area networking," then Ethernet represented the key sociotechnical system for "local area networking": a cabling and communication protocol that helped institutions "wire" themselves for a growing menu of shared digital devices. Interestingly, the development and deployment of Ethernet as an industry standard was driven less by the "paperless office" goals of sharing virtual documents and sending electronic mail, and more by the practical, material needs of sending font and layout data to a new generation of office laser printers for "what you see (on the screen) is what you get (on the page)" hard-copy production in a reasonable amount of time. In other words, the search for a fast digital network between office workstations and the workers who used them was driven, in large part, by the business norms of print culture.[24]

Mattel handheld baseball game. Image courtesy of Computer History Museum.

Constructing Cyberspace: The Internet and the World Wide Web

Since the early 1990s, the digital networks connecting corporate and personal computers have served not as a means to reproduce print culture, but as the gateway to a new communication culture often imagined as wholly distinct from print: the culture of "cyberspace." Today this term is usually understood as a synonym for the World Wide Web, especially in the spatial understanding of the web as a collection of "sites" connected by "links" and "navigated" by users. However, the term may also be applied to any electronically mediated informational environment in which social action (consumption, production, education, recreation, political participation) is fragmented across both physical and virtual space. Whether a fantasy game conducted within a virtual reality or a business transaction conducted over a telephone call, activity in cyberspace inevitably straddles both the digital and the material, implicating both mind and body.[25]

The protocols that underpin today's web began life in 1980 as "Enquire," a small program written by CERN software consultant Tim Berners-Lee "for no loftier reason than to help me remember the connections among the various people, computers, and projects at the lab."[26] Over the next decade, the community of practice within scientific computing where Berners-Lee made his career helped refine and promote a whole set of "World Wide Web" data protocols, until the turning point in 1993 when programmers Marc Andreessen and Eric Bina at the University of Illinois National Center for Supercomputing Applications built the first version of their Mosaic Web browser and made it freely available for download over the Internet.[27] The web that resulted was a space constituted out of the standard format of "Universal Resource Locator" (URL) addresses for multimedia web resources of all types (text, audio, image, video), each of which could be combined to form web "pages" linked into "sites" within named "domains" owned and managed by individual or institutional actors.

The resulting experiential geography of the web can be conceptualized as involving both places and regions, connected (and separated) both by boundaries and by paths.[28] High-value portal pages and search engines claim gatekeeper status, in which web metadata (data about other data) is used to create both human-organized entry points and algorithmically created organizational schemes for this space. Vast areas of the web requiring special access privileges—passwords, paid memberships, or institutional affiliations—mark who can and cannot travel from portal and search engine to informational node. And

Tim Berners-Lee who, with the help of Robert Cailliau, developed the World Wide Web, poses with the NeXT computer, on which he created the first web server. Courtesy CERN Document Server.

even without controlled access restrictions, one can imagine both a visible and invisible web: what can be "crawled" by an automated agent versus what must be dynamically built from off-line databases and algorithms.[29] This is a geography of code, and, as legal scholar Lawrence Lessig points out, "In cyberspace we must understand how code regulates—how the software and hardware that make cyberspace what it is regulate cyberspace as it is."[30]

Yet cyberspace is increasingly conceptualized not simply as a network of technological nodes—personal computers and web servers, cell phones and data farms—but as a network of individuals. Or, more accurately, besides being conceptualized as an "internetwork" of technological networks (a network of networks, each with its own geographical extent and institutional control), cyberspace is now conceptualized as an internetwork of human networks (a network of communities, each with its own affiliations of interest that may or may not correlate with any single physical or institutional space).[31] Sociologist Barry Wellman, for example, has argued that the recent growth of human internetworks of affiliation as practiced through technological internetworks of communication has "transformed cyberspace into cyberplaces, as people connect online with kindred spirits, engage in supportive and sociable relationships with them, and imbue their activity online with meaning, belonging and identity."[32]

This contradictory relationship sits at the at the center of the most widely known attempt to reconceptualize cyberspace in terms of urban geography: the "space of flows" thesis of urban theorist Manuel Castells.[33] In his pre-web monograph *The Informational City* (1989), Castells declared the new importance of networks of real places connected through the structures of cyberspaces: "The new international economy creates a variable geometry of production and consumption, labor and capital, management and information—a geometry that denies the specific productive meaning of any place outside its position in a network whose shape changes relentlessly in response to the messages of unseen signals and unknown codes."[34] Later in his post-web, three-volume follow-up *The Information Age* (1996–98), Castells called this relational geometry the "space of flows," and argued that it was comprised of "purposeful, repetitive, programmable sequences of exchange and interaction between physically disjointed positions held by social actors in the economic, political, and symbolic structures of society."[35] For Castells, action in cyberspace did not substitute for action in physical space; rather, it worked to rearrange the hierarchy of power within the "space of places"—meaning that firms, cities, regions, nations, and perhaps even individuals would succeed in the new global economy not if they possessed unique characteristics in physical space, but only if they could build sufficient presence in (and connections to) the new space of flows. Ironically, even the venture capitalists and technology entrepreneurs of the "dot.com" economy itself would be subject to this logic that "place matters" when building the new economy—after all, most remained concentrated in urban areas suffused with high-tech labor and capital, from Silicon Valley in

California to the Route 128 corridor in Massachusetts.[36] This space of flows has continued to evolve globally, along with both new technological possibilities and new social dynamics, especially the revolution in personal, wireless, mobile communications (cell phone conversation and wi-fi computing) that Castells and others have argued "deepens and diffuses the network society."[37]

DIGITAL CONVERGENCE AND DIGITAL DIVIDES

Just as with the rapid rise of television in the 1950s, the rapid adoption of the World Wide Web in the 1990s had consequences for nearly every other communication technology. But those consequences were neither inevitable nor obvious for the historical actors at the time. One term was applied over and over again by the new technology entrepreneurs: "digital convergence." Often this was used to mean "convergence of many different kinds of digitized media on one consumer device or appliance," such as the convergence of music-playing, video-watching, and letter-sending capabilities on personal computers. (Many schemes, from teletext in the 1980s to WebTV in the 1990s, attempted to locate the appliance of convergence in the television, but in its analog form it evaded most of these attempts.) A second understanding of "digital convergence" is perhaps more useful: The convergence of formerly distinct media firms, hardware firms, and software firms into cooperative ventures, strategic alliances, or outright mergers in an effort to reap competitive benefits from the digitalization and cross-ownership of media content and media infrastructure.[38] For example, Apple Computer changed its name simply to "Apple Inc." when it was clear that its line of personal digital music players and Internet-enabled cell phones was just as important to its brand (and its balance sheet) as its traditional desktop and laptop computers.

With these two understandings of convergence—one a commodity convergence, the other a corporate convergence—comes a third meaning of the term: the movement of social processes formerly restricted to analog media of print or broadcast into the digital realm. For example, the digital convergence of journalism with online media was alternatively hoped for as a way to invigorate an industry tainted with conservative charges of "liberal bias," and feared as a death knell for locally produced investigative journalism in favor of nationally syndicated "lifestyle news."[39] As Pablo J. Boczkowski demonstrated in his study *Digitizing the News*, newspaper owners large and small were experimenting with various futures all through the late 1980s and early 1990s, convinced that change was coming but unsure of their position in a world of supposedly user-customizable online news content and micro-targeted online news advertising.[40] As with previous communication changes, users upset the best-laid plans of the media producers: the idiosyncratic production and consumption of weblogs which began shortly before the turn of the millennium caught newspaper owners by surprise, even as those weblogs made more intensive use of any and all firsthand reporting they could access (usually for free) through the mainstream media.

These initial consequences of institutional and technological convergence within cyberspace have too often carried with them the idea that neither material place nor national power matter any more.[41] Sometimes this is linked to a utopian telecommuting and "electronic cottage" vision of decentralized producers and consumers interacting from individual, isolated households in some sort of "virtual community." Other times it is tied to a neoliberal globalization analysis that claims that nation-states do not, and should not, matter to the transnational flow of information (and, by extension, financial capital)—visions of "friction-free capitalism" in a "demassified" cyberspace.[42] But even successful e-commerce ventures such as eBay, while allowing global markets for obscure goods (and communities of consumption around these goods) to emerge that transcend material space, still depend on place-based transportation networks and state-based regulations concerning shipping fraud. Philosopher of technology Langdon Winner, referring to such free-market cyberspace dreams as "sociopathic cyberlibertarianism," has called for greater connections between global cyberspaces and local, small-scale interest and action groups as a way to orient cyberspace not only to the individual demands of consumption, but to the collective needs of a citizenry.[43]

It is not simply corporations and consumers who might inhabit this cyberspace, but workers at well.[44] At one end of the wage scale, the highly skilled programmers and designers of the once-booming "e-commerce" sector are starting to question their stock-option-laden compensation packages in a market where the inevitable initial public offering is no longer an automatic road to riches. At the other end, many of the lower-paid workers at "e-tailers" such as Amazon.com—not only stock checkers walking the halls of warehouses, but technicians monitoring back-office server farms and temporary workers staffing technical-support phone lines—are demanding the right to unionize in pursuit of better wages, better hours, and more secure jobs. And somewhere in between, a so-called "long tail" of decentralized, independent, part-time, small-scale merchants and resellers and consultants attempt to connect their goods and services to an equally diffuse and idiosyncratic consumer market through the new default storefront of cyberspace: one's crucial and often volatile position on the first page of a Google search. In all of these ways, the new virtual economy cannot escape a very old physical fact: it takes human labor to make the web work.[45]

Research focused on the social relations of cyberspace in terms of political-economic power has revealed deep and continuing disparities in how cyberspace is entered, experienced, and imagined across the globe. As initial mappings of cyberspace repeatedly revealed highly uneven and sometimes polarized patterns of connectivity, accessibility, and usability over urban space, researchers began to address questions of social justice, exclusion, and diversity within the geography of cyberspace, often under the concept of a "digital divide."[46] Tied as they are to a preexisting and uneven global urban geography, connections into cyberspace and the key characteristics of those connections (bandwidth, quality, cost) are unequally distributed in real space (especially with respect to poorer cities, regions, and nation-states). Pippa Norris has argued that such barriers work at three different geographic and social scales: "A global divide is evident between industrialized and developing societies. A social divide is apparent between rich and poor within each nation. And within the online community, evidence for a democratic divide is emerging between those who do and those who do not use Internet resources to engage, mobilize, and participate in public life."[47] The perpetually innovative nature of cyberspace seems to ensure that even as one technological landscape is normalized (dial-up online connectivity), another one with higher consumer, labor, and infrastructure costs takes its place (fiber-optic broadband connectivity).

Yet cyberspace encompasses not only digital divides, but also digital differences. Sherry Turkle's influential 1995 book *Life on the Screen* explored what was then a cutting-edge version of cyberspace: simultaneous, multi-user textual gaming environments referred to as "MUDs" (Multi-User Dungeons, reflecting the fantasy-literature origins of the practice) or "MOOs" (MUDs Object Oriented, reflecting the ability of users to create their own objects and areas within the MUD). She demonstrated that exploring social action in cyberspace also meant exploring the psychology and sociology of identity formation as mediated by information technology.[48] Her work raised questions about gender differences in cognitive behavior, about holistic identity versus fragmented and contradictory identity, and about the process of identity formation through simulation, play, and communication. Scaling up these concerns to focus on social groups rather than individuals, cultural-studies research has begun to ask whether cyberspace is experienced, understood, and produced differently from different positionalities not only relating to geography and class, but also race, ethnicity, gender, and age.[49]

In all of these cases, whether in exposing digital divides or acknowledging digital differences, researchers have found it useful to consider cyberspace not as a neutral geography which is "given" as a realm for social action through value-free technological innovation, but as a contested space whose form and meanings are themselves produced and reproduced by diverse social actors with diverse social goals. And this is a definition which holds true whether that cyberspace is thought of historically as a space of web sites and 3D games, or as a space of telephone calls and television programs.

CONCLUSION
INFORMATION SOCIETIES AND GLOBAL CHALLENGES

This story of communication technology that started with physical inscriptions on paper, moved to electrical signals through wires and waves, and now incorporates a digital mix of hyperlinked multimedia circulating through an ever-growing cyberspace, leaves us in a paradoxical situation. Our technological information/communication infrastructure—still not fully global or universal, but bringing more kinds of information to more individuals, households, and businesses at more hours of the day than ever before—has created what media critic Todd Gitlin calls a state of "unlimited media": "a torrent of immense force and constancy, an accompaniment to life that has become a central experience of life."[1] Yet at the same time, many of us feel overwhelmed, supersaturated, and woefully underinformed about the world in which we live. No recent media event in the United States captured this paradox as clearly as the September 11, 2001, terrorist attacks, a media event not only because most of the nation experienced the attacks (and the subsequent wars waged in their name) through mediated technologies of print, radio, television, and Internet, but also because the very purpose and power of terrorism itself is to create a media spectacle that is impossible to ignore.[2]

In the first hours after the attacks, mainstream news sites operating over the web seemed to have reached their limits of operation—the *New York Times* removed graphics and advertising in order to serve pages more quickly, and

New York City, September 11, 2001. The destruction of the World Trade Center cast into stark relief the complexities and contradictions inherent in modern global communication.

Google actually posted a warning message: "If you are looking for news, you will find the most current information on TV or radio." On the other hand, non-news sites such as the technology-enthusiast hangout Slashdot stepped up to relay news from TV, the wire services, and e-mails from users. And countless new "weblogs" (web-based logs of news and musings of all sorts) mobilized to offer "eyewitness accounts, personal photographs, and in some cases video footage" that were used by overworked journalists as leads to follow up for print and broadcast media stories.[3] Yet when the initial panic had subsided, we were left with media scholar James Carey's sober assessment: "The news media, the political class, intellectuals—all the distant and early warning systems of the culture—had failed and Americans were left baffled, muttering questions like 'What is going on in the world? Who were these people anyway? What went wrong?' Or, most plaintively, 'Why don't they like us?'"[4] Time did not correct the failure; broadcasting historian Susan Douglas noted that:

> After 9/11, when one would have expected the nightly news programs to provide a greater focus on international news, attention to the rest of the world was fleeting, with the exception of the war in Iraq. After a precipitous decline in celebrity and lifestyle news in the immediate aftermath of the 9/11 catastrophe, a year later the percentages of these stories in the nightly news were back to where they had been pre-9/11. In 2004, despite the war, the percentage of stories about foreign affairs on the commercial nightly news broadcasts was lower than it had been in 1997.[5]

Perhaps, as media theorist Robert McChesney has argued, "corporate concentration, conglomeration, and hypercommercialism" in the mass communication industries had caused "the corruption and degradation of journalism, to the point where it is scarcely a democratic force."[6] Yet if this is so, it was happen-

Inauguration Day, January 20, 2009. The election of Barack Obama, the first African American president, owed a lot to "Web 2.0" technologies. Photo by Bob Korn.

ing even as the state itself mobilized all the tools of strategic communications media campaigns in the mass media to build up support for a war of choice in Iraq on pretenses of technological fear—weapons of mass destruction—which proved to be illusory.[7]

It is easy to blame media firms, media technologies, or even whole media ecologies, in the face of such failures. It was during the height of the Cold War under the Reagan/Bush administration that Neil Postman argued that "under the governance of the printing press, discourse in America was different from what it is now—generally coherent, serious and rational" but "under the governance of television, it has become shriveled and absurd."[8] But that's too simple a diagnosis. In an age of web-based media that are highly textual, clearly the absence of text is not our problem—nor has the preponderance of text created an utopia. So-called "Web 2.0" technologies—combining digital infrastructures, social networks, and freely offered public labor in creating and organizing digital content—certainly have not provided the participatory democracy that many may have hoped for.[9] Web 2.0 has not been able to bring peace in the "War on Terror." But it was instrumental in the mobilization of youth during the presidential campaign that elected the first African American to the White House in 2008. And through a controversial online whistleblower document site known as "WikiLeaks," the amateur participatory energy of Web 2.0, coupled with professional reporting and analysis from the still-relevant print and broadcast media, may at least remind us that our current "long wars" demand serious and sustained attention and concern from an audience all-too-ready to move on to happier distractions.

Communication technology has always been wrapped up, not only in profound political, economic, and social change itself, but in the ways in which we recognize, criticize, and celebrate such historic changes as well. In a nation like the United States, we demand much from our infrastructures of communication: they must provide a means to bind together states and cities, corporations and collectivities, across space and time; they must provide a forum for the mediation of competing interests, not only between political right and left, but among an ever-changing multicultural mix of histories and dreams; and they must function adequately under the ever-present tension of promoting the collective public interest while preserving the accumulation of private profit. The study of the history of communication technology in America is never free of these competing demands either—nor, thankfully, is it ever complete.

NOTES

INTRODUCTION

1. Frances Cairncross, *The Death of Distance: How the Communications Revolution Is Changing Our Lives* (Cambridge, Mass.: Harvard Business School Press, 1997).

2. Paul Starr, *The Creation of the Media: Political Origins of Modern Communications* (New York: Basic Books, 2004).

3. Allan R. Pred, *Urban Growth and the Circulation of Information: The United States System of Cities, 1790–1840* (Cambridge, Mass.: Harvard University Press, 1973), 61, 144.

4. Robert C. Post, *Technology, Transport, and Travel in American History* (Washington, D.C.: Society for the History of Technology/American Historical Association, 2003).

5. Richard R. John, *Network Nation: Inventing American Telecommunications* (Cambridge, Mass.: Belknap Press, 2010).

6. William Cronon, *Nature's Metropolis: Chicago and the Great West* (New York: W.W. Norton & Co., 1991). See also Stephen H. Cutcliffe, "Classics Revisited— "Travels in and Out of Town: William Cronon's *Nature's Metropolis: Chicago and the Great West,*" *Technology and Culture* 51 (2010): 728–37.

7. Alfred D. Chandler Jr., *The Visible Hand: The Managerial Revolution in American Business* (Cambridge, Mass.: Belknap Press, 1977); David Montgomery, *Workers' Control in America: Studies in the History of Work, Technology, and Labor Struggles* (New York: Cambridge University Press, 1979); Oliver Zunz, *Making America Corporate: 1870–1920* (Chicago: University of Chicago Press, 1990).

8. Quoted in Carolyn Marvin, *When Old Technologies Were New: Thinking about Electric Communication in the Late Nineteenth Century* (New York: Oxford University Press, 1988), 192.

9. James L. Baughman, *The Republic of Mass Culture: Journalism, Filmmaking, and Broadcasting in America since 1941* (Baltimore: Johns Hopkins University Press, 2006); Amy Sue Bix, *Inventing Ourselves Out of Jobs? America's Debate over Technological Unemployment, 1929–1981* (Baltimore: Johns Hopkins University Press, 2000).

10. Nicholas Negroponte, *Being Digital* (New York: Knopf, 1995), 12.

11. Lisa Gitelman, *Always Already New: New Media, History, and the Data of Culture* (Cambridge, Mass.: MIT Press, 2006).

12. Robert MacDougall, "The Wire Devils: Pulp Thrillers, the Telephone, and Action at a Distance in the Wiring of a Nation," *American Quarterly* 57 (2006): 715–41.

13. Tarleton Gillespie, *Wired Shut: Copyright and the Shape of Digital Culture* (Cambridge, Mass.: MIT Press, 2007).

14. William Hoynes, *Public Television For Sale: Media, the Market, and the Public Sphere* (Boulder, Colo.: Westview Press, 1994).

15. Deborah Brandt, *Literacy in American Lives* (New York: Cambridge University Press, 2001).

16. Ben Bagdikian, *The New Media Monopoly* (Boston: Beacon Press, 2004).

17. Manuel Castells, Mireia Fernandez-Ardevol, Jack Linchuan Qiu, and Araba Sey, *Mobile Communication and Society: A Global Perspective* (Cambridge, Mass.: MIT Press, 2006).

18. Charles R. Acland, ed., *Residual Media* (Minneapolis: University of Minnesota Press, 2007).

19. On the history of technology in the U.S., especially useful are Ruth Schwartz Cowan, *A Social History of American Technology* (New York: Oxford University Press, 1997) and Carroll Pursell, ed., *A Companion to American Technology* (Malden, Mass.: Blackwell, 2005).

20. For an introduction to the study of media and technological infrastructure, see: Edward S. Herman and Robert W. McChesney, *The Global Media: The New Missionaries of Corporate Capitalism* (London: Cassell, 1997); Paul Edwards, "Y2K: Millennial Reflections on Computers as Infrastructure," *History and Technology* 15 (1998): 7–29; Geoffrey C. Bowker and Susan Leigh Star, *Sorting Things Out: Classification and Its Consequences* (Cambridge, Mass.: MIT Press, 1999); and Stephen Graham and Simon Marvin, *Splintering Urbanism: Networked Infrastructures, Technological Mobilities and the Urban Condition* (New York: Routledge, 2001).

21. Paul Edwards, "Infrastructure and Modernity: Force, Time, and Social Organization in the History of Sociotechnical Systems," in *Modernity and Technology,* ed. Thomas J. Misa, Philip Brey, and Andrew Feenberg (Cambridge, Mass.: MIT Press, 2003).

22. Thomas Hughes, *Networks of Power: Electrification in Western Society, 1880–1930* (Baltimore: Johns Hopkins University Press, 1985).

23. Ruth Schwartz Cowan, *More Work for Mother: The Ironies of Household Technology from the Open Hearth to the Microwave* (New York: Basic Books, 1983).

24. Langdon Winner, *The Whale and the Reactor: A Search for Limits in an Age of High Technology* (Chicago: University of Chicago Press, 1986); Wiebe E. Bijker, Thomas Parke Hughes, and Trevor J. Pinch, eds., *The Social Construction of Technological Systems: New Directions in the Sociology and History of Technology* (Cambridge, Mass.:

MIT Press, 1987); Donald MacKenzie and Judy Wajcman, eds., *The Social Shaping of Technology*, 2nd ed. (Philadelphia: Open University Press, 1999).

25. Harold D. Lasswell, "The Structure and Function of Communication in Society," in *The Communication of Ideas,* ed. Lyman Bryson (New York: Cooper Square, 1964), 37–38.

26. James W. Carey, "A Cultural Approach to Communication," *Communication* 2, no. 2 (1975): 1–22.

27. Stephen Graham and Simon Marvin, *Telecommunications and the City: Electronic Spaces, Urban Places* (New York: Routledge, 1996).

28. Alvin Toffler, *The Third Wave* (New York: Morrow, 1980).

29. Manuel Castells, *The Informational City: Information Technology, Economic Restructuring, and the Urban-Regional Process* (New York: Blackwell, 1989).

30. Saskia Sassen, *Cities in a World Economy* (Thousand Oaks, Calif.: Pine Forge Press, 1994).

31. William Mitchell, *City of Bits: Space, Place, and the Infobahn* (Cambridge, Mass.: MIT Press, 1995).

32. James O. Wheeler, Yuko Aoyama, and Barney Warf, eds., *Cities in the Telecommunications Age: The Fracturing of Geographies* (New York: Routledge, 2000).

33. Mark E. Hepworth, *Geography of the Information Economy* (New York: The Guilford Press, 1990); Aharon Kellerman, *Telecommunications and Geography* (London: Belhaven 1993).

34. Donald G. Janelle, "Global Interdependence and Its Consequences," in *Collapsing Space and Time: Geographic Aspects of Communication and Information*, ed. Stanley D. Brunn and Thomas R. Leinbach (London: HarperCollins Academic, 1991), 49–81, quotation on 49.

35. David Harvey, *The Condition of Postmodernity: An Enquiry into the Origins of Cultural Change* (Cambridge, Mass.: Blackwell, 1989), 255.

36. For example: Stephen Lubar, *Infoculture: The Smithsonian Book of Information Age Inventions* (Boston: Houghton Mifflin, 1993); Brian Winston, *Media Technology and Society: A History from the Telegraph to the Internet* (Routledge: New York, 1998); Alfred D. Chandler Jr. and James W. Cortada, eds., *A Nation Transformed by Information: How Information has Shaped the United States from Colonial Times to the Present* (New York: Oxford University Press, 2000).

37. Marshall McLuhan, *Understanding Media: The Extensions of Man* (New York: New American Library, 1964).

38. Merritt Roe Smith and Leo Marx, eds., *Does Technology Drive History? The Dilemma of Technological Determinism* (Cambridge, Mass.: MIT Press, 1994).

CHAPTER 1

1. Walter J. Ong, S.J., *Orality and Literacy: The Technologizing of the Word* (New York: Methuen, 1982).

2. Jack Goody, *The Interface between the Written and the Oral* (New York: Cambridge University Press, 1987). See also David R. Olson and Michael Cole, eds., *Technology, Literacy, and the Evolution of Society: Implications of the Work of Jack Goody* (Mahwah, N.J.: Lawrence Erlbaum, 2006).

3. Neil Postman, *Amusing Ourselves to Death: Public Discourse in the Age of Show Business* (New York: Penguin Books, 1985).

4. Deborah Brandt, *Literacy in American Lives* (New York: Cambridge University Press, 2001).

5. See Elizabeth Eisenstein, *The Printing Press as an Agent of Change: Communications and Cultural Transformations in Early Modern Europe,* 2 vols. (New York: Cambridge University Press, 1979); Adrian Johns, *The Nature of the Book: Print and Knowledge in the Making* (Chicago: University of Chicago Press, 1998); and the debate between these two scholars in the February 2002 issue of the *American Historical Review,* 87–128.

6. Stephan Füssel, *Gutenberg and the Impact of Printing* (Burlington, Vt.: Ashgate, 2005); Jonathan M. Bloom, *Paper before Print: The History and Impact of Paper in the Islamic World* (New Haven: Yale University Press, 2001).

7. Paul Saenger, *Space between Words: The Origins of Silent Reading* (Stanford: Stanford University Press, 1997); Kevin Sharpe and Steven N. Zwicker, eds., *Reading, Society and Politics in Early Modern England* (New York: Cambridge University Press, 2003).

8. Thomas Augst, introduction to *Institutions of Reading: The Social Life of Libraries in the United States,* ed. Thomas Augst and Kenneth Carpenter (Amherst: University of Massachusetts Press, 2007), 1–21, quotation on 4.

9. Richard D. Brown, *Knowledge Is Power: The Diffusion of Information in Early America, 1700–1865* (New York: Oxford University Press, 1989); Richard D. Brown, "Early American Origins of the Information Age," in *A Nation Transformed by Information: How Information Has Shaped the United States from Colonial Times to the Present,* ed. Alfred D. Chandler Jr. and James W. Cortada (New York: Oxford University Press, 2000), 39–53, quotation on 42.

10. Harvey Graff, *The Legacies of Literacy: Continuities and Contradictions in Western Culture and Society* (Bloomington: Indiana University Press, 1991), 164.

11. Hugh Amory and David D. Hall, eds., *A History of the Book in America,* vol. 1. (Chapel Hill: University of North Carolina Press, 2007).

12. Ross W. Beales and E. Jennifer Monaghan, "Literacy and Schoolbooks," in *A History of the Book in America,* vol. 1, ed. Amory and Hall, 1:380–87, quotation on 382.

13. David D. Hall, introduction to *A History of the Book in America*, vol. 1, ed. Amory and Hall, 1:1–25.

14. Ronald J. Zboray and Mary Saracino Zboray, *Literary Dollars and Social Sense: A People's History of the Mass Market Book* (New York: Routledge, 2005), xvii.

15. Brown, "Early American Origins of the Information Age," 40.

16. James Raven, *London Booksellers and American Customers: Transatlantic Literary Community and the Charleston Library Society, 1748–1811* (Columbia: University of South Carolina Press, 2002); Rosalind Remer, *Printers and Men of Capital: Philadelphia Book Publishers in the New Republic* (Philadelphia: University of Pennsylvania Press, 1996).

17. Candy Gunther Brown, *The Word in the World: Evangelical Writing, Publishing, and Reading in America, 1789–1880* (Chapel Hill: University of North Carolina Press, 2004); Zboray and Zboray, *Literary Dollars and Social Sense*.

18. David M. Henkin, *City Reading: Written Words and Public Spaces in Antebellum New York* (New York: Columbia University Press, 1998).

19. Hugh Amory, "Reinventing the Colonial Book," in *A History of the Book in America*, ed. Amory and Hall, 1:26–54.

20. Judith A. McGaw, *Most Wonderful Machine: Mechanization and Social Change in Berkshire Paper Making, 1801–1995* (Princeton, N.J.: Princeton University Press, 1987).

21. Tamara Plakins Thornton, *Handwriting in America: A Cultural History* (New Haven: Yale University Press, 1996).

22. Margery Davies, *Woman's Place Is at the Typewriter: Office Work and Office Workers, 1870–1930* (Philadelphia: Temple University Press, 1982).

23. Gregory J. Downey, *Closed Captioning: Subtitling, Stenography, and the Digital Convergence of Text with Television* (Baltimore: Johns Hopkins University Press, 2008).

24. See Michael Schudson "News, Public, Nation," *American Historical Review* 107 (2002): 481–95.

25. David Paul Nord, *Communities of Journalism: A History of American Newspapers and their Readers* (Urbana: University of Illinois Press, 2001).

26. Richard R. John, *Spreading the News: The American Postal System from Franklin to Morse* (Cambridge, Mass.: Harvard University Press, 1995), quotation on 38.

---

27. Gerald J. Baldasty, "The Rise of News as a Commodity: Business Imperatives and the Press in the Nineteenth Century," in *Ruthless Criticism: New Perspectives in U.S. Communication History,* ed. William S. Solomon and Robert W. McChesney (Minneapolis: University of Minnesota Press, 1993), 98–121, quote on 99.

28. Jürgen Habermas, *The Structural Transformation of the Public Sphere: An Inquiry into a Category of Bourgeois Society* (Cambridge, Mass.: MIT Press, 1989).

29. Benedict Anderson, *Imagined Communities: Reflections on the Origin and Spread of Nationalism* (London: Verso, 1983).

30. Gary Bryan Magee, *Productivity and Performance in the Paper Industry: Labour, Capital, and Technology in Britain and America, 1860–1914* (Cambridge: Cambridge University Press, 1997).

31. Walker Rumble, *The Swifts: Printers in the Age of Typesetting Races* (Charlottesville: University of Virginia Press, 2003).

32. Aurora Wallace, *Newspapers and the Making of Modern America: A History* (Westport, Conn.: Greenwood Press, 2005).

33. Michael Schudson, *Discovering the News: A Social History of American Newspapers* (New York: Basic Books, 1978), quotations on 90.

34. James P. Danky and Wayne A. Wiegand, eds., *Print Culture in a Diverse America* (Urbana: University of Illinois Press, 1998).

35. Elizabeth McHenry, *Forgotten Readers: Recovering the Lost History of African American Literary Societies* (Durham, N.C.: Duke University Press, 2002).

36. Reese V. Jenkins, "Technology and the Market: George Eastman and the Origins of Mass Amateur Photography," in *Technology and American History: A Historical Anthology from Technology & Culture,* ed. Stephen H. Cutcliffe and Terry S. Reynolds (Chicago: University of Chicago Press, 1997), 197–215.

37. Jenkins, "Technology and the Market," 212.

38. Joshua Brown, *Beyond the Lines: Pictorial Reporting, Everyday Life, and the Crisis of Gilded Age America* (Berkeley: University of California Press, 2002); Carolyn Kitch, *The Girl on the Magazine Cover: The Origins of Visual Stereotypes in American Mass Media* (Chapel Hill: University of North Carolina Press, 2001); Richard Dyer, "Making 'White' People White," in *The Social Shaping of Technology,* ed. Donald MacKenzie and Judy Wajcman, 2d ed. (Philadelphia: Open University Press, 1999).

39. Mary Panzer, *Mathew Brady and the Image of History* (Washington, D.C.: Smithsonian Books, 1997); Jacob A. Riis, *How the Other Half Lives: Studies among the Tenements of New York* (Boston: Bedford Books, 1996).

40. Marc Olivier, "George Eastman's Modern Stone-Age Family: Snapshot Photography and the Brownie," *Technology and Culture* 48 (2007): 1–19, quotation on 2.

---

41. Mary Warner Marien, *Photography and Its Critics: A Cultural History, 1839–1900* (Cambridge: Cambridge University Press, 1998).

42. Edward M. Lenert, "A Communication Theory Perspective on Telecommunications Policy," *Journal of Communication* 48 (1998): 3–23, quotation on 14.

43. John Lauritz Larson, *Internal Improvement: National Public Works and the Promise of Popular Government in the Early United States* (Chapel Hill: University of North Carolina Press, 2001).

44. John, *Spreading the News*; David M. Henkin, *The Postal Age: The Emergence of Modern Communications in Nineteenth-Century America* (Chicago: University of Chicago Press, 2006).

45. Wayne E Fuller, *Morality and the Mail in Nineteenth-Century America* (Champaign: University of Illinois Press, 2003).

46. On the history of libraries in the United States, see Wayne A. Wiegand and Donald G. Davis, eds., *Encyclopedia of Library History* (New York: Garland, 1994) and Wiegand, "Tunnel Vision and Blind Spots: Reflections on the Twentieth-Century History of American Librarianship," *Library Quarterly* 69 (1999): 1–32.

47. Carl Ostrowski, *Books, Maps, and Politics: A Cultural History of the Library of Congress, 1783–1861* (Amherst: University of Massachusetts Press, 2004).

48. Isabelle Lehuu, *Carnival on the Page: Popular Print Media in Antebellum America* (Chapel Hill: University of North Carolina Press, 2000).

49. Dee Garrison, *Apostles of Culture: The Public Librarian and American Society, 1876–1920* (New York: Free Press, 1979).

50. Siva Vaidhyanathan, *Copyrights and Copywrongs: The Rise of Intellectual Property and How It Threatens Creativity* (New York: New York University Press, 2001).

51. Tarleton Gillespie, *Wired Shut: Copyright and the Shape of Digital Culture* (Cambridge, Mass.: MIT Press, 2007).

CHAPTER 2

1. Margo J. Anderson, *The American Census: A Social History* (New Haven, Conn.: Yale University Press, 1988).

2. Gary Fields, *Territories of Profit: Communications, Capitalist Development, and the Innovative Enterprises of G. F. Swift and Dell Computer* (Stanford: Stanford University Press, 2003).

3. James R. Beniger, *The Control Revolution: Technological and Economic Origins of the Information Society* (Cambridge, Mass.: Harvard University Press, 1986).

4. Stephen Kern, *The Culture of Time and Space, 1880–1918* (Cambridge, Mass.: Harvard University Press, 1983).

5. JoAnne Yates, *Control through Communication: The Rise of System in American Management* (Baltimore: Johns Hopkins University Press, 1989).

6. William Cronon, *Nature's Metropolis: Chicago and the Great West* (New York: W.W. Norton & Co., 1991).

7. Gerald W. Brock, *The Second Information Revolution* (Cambridge, Mass.: Harvard University Press, 2003).

8. Paul Israel, *From Machine Shop to Industrial Laboratory: Telegraphy and the Changing Context of American Invention, 1830–1920* (Baltimore: Johns Hopkins University Press, 1992).

9. Tom Wheeler, *Mr. Lincoln's T-Mails: The Untold Story of How Abraham Lincoln Used the Telegraph to Win the Civil War* (New York: HarperCollins, 2006).

10. Tom Standage, *The Victorian Internet: The Remarkable Story of the Telegraph and the Nineteenth Century's On-Line Pioneers* (New York: Walker and Company, 1998).

11. Dwayne R. Winseck and Robert M. Pike, *Communication and Empire: Media, Markets, and Globalization, 1860–1930* (Durham, N.C.: Duke University Press, 2007); Edwin Gabler, *The American Telegrapher: A Social History, 1860–1900* (New Brunswick: Rutgers University Press, 1988); Joel A. Tarr with Thomas Finholt and David Goodman, "The City and the Telegraph: Urban Telecommunications in the Pre-Telephone Era," *Journal of Urban History* 14 (1987): 38–80.

12. Richard R. John, "Recasting the Information Infrastructure for the Industrial Age," in *A Nation Transformed by Information: How Information Has Shaped the United States from Colonial Times to the Present,* ed. Alfred D. Chandler Jr. and James W. Cortada (New York: Oxford University Press, 2000), 55–106.

13. Robert MacDougall, "The Wire Devils: Pulp Thrillers, the Telephone, and Action at a Distance in the Wiring of a Nation," *American Quarterly* 57 (2006): 715–41, quotation on 716.

14. Claude S. Fischer, *America Calling: A Social History of the Telephone to 1940* (Berkeley: University of California Press, 1992).

15. Menahem Blondheim, *News Over the Wires: The Telegraph and the Flow of Public Information in America, 1844–1897* (Cambridge, Mass.: Harvard University Press, 1994), 3.

16. Robert MacDougall, "The People's Telephone: The Politics of Telephony in the United States and Canada," *Enterprise and Society* 6 (2005): 581–87.

17. Milton L. Mueller Jr., *Universal Service: Competition, Interconnection, and Monopoly in the Making of the American Telephone System* (Cambridge, Mass.: MIT Press, 1997).

18. Thomas P. Hughes, *American Genesis: A Century of Invention and Technological Enthusiasm, 1870–1970* (New York: Viking, 1989).

19. Alfred D. Chandler Jr., *The Visible Hand: The Managerial Revolution in American Business* (Cambridge, Mass.: Belknap Press, 1977).

20. Gerald W. Brock, *The Telecommunications Industry: The Dynamics of Market Structure* (Cambridge, Mass.: Harvard University Press, 1981).

21. Gabler, *The American Telegrapher*; Thomas C. Jepsen, *My Sisters Telegraphic: Women in the Telegraph Office, 1846–1950* (Athens: Ohio University Press, 2000); Gregory J. Downey, *Telegraph Messenger Boys: Labor, Technology, and Geography, 1850–1950* (New York: Routledge, 2002).

22. Amy Sue Bix, *Inventing Ourselves Out of Jobs? America's Debate over Technological Unemployment, 1929–1981* (Baltimore: Johns Hopkins University Press, 2000).

23. Venus Green, *Race on the Line: Gender, Labor, and Technology in the Bell System, 1880–1980* (Durham, N.C.: Duke University Press, 2001).

24. James B. Murray Jr., *Wireless Nation: The Frenzied Launch of the Cellular Revolution in America* (Cambridge, Mass.: Perseus, 2001).

25. Manuel Castells, Mireia Fernandez-Ardevol, Jack Linchuan Qiu, and Araba Sey, *Mobile Communication and Society: A Global Perspective* (Cambridge, Mass.: MIT Press, 2006).

CHAPTER 3

1. Paul Israel, *Edison: A Life of Invention* (New York: John Wiley and Sons, 1998); Neil Baldwin, *Edison: Inventing the Century* (New York: Hyperion, 1995); Reese V. Jenkins, "Words, Images, Artifacts and Sound: Documents for the History of Technology," *British Journal of the History of Science* 20 (1987): 39–56.

2. Robert Sklar, *Movie-made America: A Cultural History of American Movies*, 2d ed. (New York: Vintage, 1994); Douglas Gomery, *Shared Pleasures: A History of Movie Presentation in the United States* (Madison: University of Wisconsin Press, 1992).

3. Michael Denning, *Mechanic Accents: Dime Novels and Working-Class Culture in America*, revised ed. (New York: Verso, 1998); Robert H. Wiebe, *The Search for Order, 1877–1920* (New York: Hill and Wang, 1967).

4. Daniel Czitrom, *Media and the American Mind: From Morse to McLuhan* (Chapel Hill: University of North Carolina Press, 1982); David Nasaw, *Children of the City: At Work and At Play* (New York: Oxford University Press 1985).

5. Gomery, *Shared Pleasures*; Donald Crafton, *The Talkies: American Cinema's Transition to Sound, 1926–1931* (New York: Scribner, 1997); Douglas Gomery, *The Coming of Sound: A History* (New York: Routledge, 2005).

6. Emily Thompson, *The Soundscape of Modernity: Architectural Acoustics and the Culture of Listening in America, 1900–1933* (Cambridge, Mass.: MIT Press, 2002).

7. James P. Kraft, *Stage to Studio: Musicians and the Sound Revolution, 1890–1950* (Baltimore: Johns Hopkins University Press, 1996).

8. Jonathan Sterne, *The Audible Past: Cultural Origins of Sound Reproduction* (Durham, N.C.: Duke University Press, 2003).

9. David Morton, *Off the Record: The Technology and Culture of Sound Recording in America* (New Brunswick: Rutgers University Press, 2000).

10. Susan J. Douglas, *Inventing American Broadcasting, 1899–1922* (Baltimore: Johns Hopkins University Press, 1987); Susan J. Douglas, *Listening In: Radio and the American Imagination, from Amos 'n' Andy and Edward R. Murrow to Wolfman Jack and Howard Stern* (New York: Times Books, 1999).

11. Robert W. McChesney, *Rich Media, Poor Democracy* (New York: New Press, 2000).

12. Margaret Graham, "The Threshold of the Information Age: Radio, Television, and Motion Pictures Mobilize the Nation," in *A Nation Transformed by Information: How Information has Shaped the United States from Colonial Times to the Present,* ed. Alfred D. Chandler Jr. and James W. Cortada (New York: Oxford University Press, 2000), 137–75.

13. Douglas, *Listening In,* 56.

14. Kathy Newman, *Radio Active: Advertising and Consumer Activism, 1935–1947* (Berkeley: University of California Press, 2004).

15. Gerald Nachman, *Raised on Radio* (New York: Pantheon Books, 1998).

16. Raymond Williams, *Television: Technology and Cultural Form* (New York: Schocken, 1975).

17. Erik Barnouw, *Tube of Plenty: The Evolution of American Television,* 2d ed. (New York: Oxford University Press, 1990).

18. Graham, "The Threshold of the Information Age."

19. David Weinstein, *The Forgotten Network: DuMont and the Birth of American Television* (Philadelphia: Temple University Press, 2004).

20. Robert J. Blakely, *To Serve the Public Interest: Educational Broadcasting in the United States* (Syracuse: Syracuse University Press, 1979).

21. Carnegie Commission on Educational Television, *Public Television: A Program for Action* (New York: Bantam, 1967), 3.

22. James L. Baughman, *The Republic of Mass Culture: Journalism, Filmmaking, and Broadcasting in America since 1941* (Baltimore: Johns Hopkins University Press, 2006), quotation on xiii.

23. Lynn Spigel, *Make Room for TV: Television and the Family Ideal in Postwar America* (Chicago: University of Chicago Press, 1992), 37.

24. Catherine Gudis, *Buyways: Billboards, Automobiles, and the American Landscape* (New York: Routledge, 2003).

25. Richard Butsch, *The Making of American Audiences: From Stage to Television, 1750–1990* (New York: Cambridge University Press, 2000), 2.

26. James Schultz, *The Romance of Small-Town Chautauquas* (Columbia: University of Missouri Press, 2002).

27. Deborah Brandt, *Literacy in American Lives* (New York: Cambridge University Press, 2001).

28. Butsch, *The Making of American Audiences*, 2.

29. Frederick Winslow Taylor, *The Principles of Scientific Management* (New York: Harper & Brothers, 1911); Harry Braverman, *Labor and Monopoly Capital: The Degradation of Work in the Twentieth Century* (New York: Monthly Review Press, 1974); Robert Kanigel, *The One Best Way: Frederick Winslow Taylor and the Enigma of Efficiency* (New York: Viking, 1997).

30. Dan Schiller, *Theorizing Communication: A History* (New York: Oxford University Press, 1996).

31. Walter Lippmann, *Public Opinion* (New York: Harcourt Brace, 1922), 32.

32. Edward L. Bernays, *Propaganda* (New York: H. Liveright, 1928), 37.

33. Harold D. Lasswell, "The Structure and Function of Communication in Society," in *The Communication of Ideas,* ed. Lyman Bryson (New York: Cooper Square, 1964), 37–38.

34. Ien Ang, "The Nature of the Audience," in *Questioning the Media: A Critical Introduction*, ed. John Downing, Ali Mohammadi, and Annabelle Sreberny-Mohammadi, 2d ed. (Thousand Oaks, Calif.: SAGE, 1995), 207–20.

35. Stuart Ewen, *Captains of Consciousness: Advertising and the Social Roots of Consumer Culture* (New York: McGraw-Hill, 1976); James B. Twitchell, *Adcult USA: The Triumph of Advertising in American Culture* (New York: Columbia University Press, 1996); Pamela Walker Laird, *Advertising Progress: American Business and the Rise of Consumer Marketing* (Baltimore: Johns Hopkins University Press, 1998).

36. Jackson Lears, *Fables of Abundance: A Cultural History of Advertising in America* (New York: Basic Books, 1994), 212.

37. Joseph Turow, *Breaking up America: Advertisers and the New Media World* (Chicago: University of Chicago Press, 1997), 57.

38. Oscar H. Gandy, Jr., "Tracking the Audience: Personal Information and Privacy," in *Questioning the Media*, ed. Downing et al., 221–37, quotation on 226.

39. Dallas Smythe, *Dependency Road: Communications, Capitalism, Consciousness, and Canada* (Norwood, N.J.: Ablex, 1981).

40. Gandy, "Tracking the Audience," 228.

41. Douglas Craig, *Fireside Politics: Radio and Political Culture in the United States, 1920–1940* (Baltimore: Johns Hopkins University Press, 2000).

42. William Boddy, "Television Begins," in *Television: An International History*, ed. Anthony Smith (New York: Oxford University Press, 1995), 35.

43. Hugh R. Slotten, *Radio and Television Regulation: Broadcast Technology in the United States, 1920–1960* (Baltimore: Johns Hopkins University Press, 2000).

44. William Hoynes, *Public Television For Sale: Media, the Market, and the Public Sphere* (Boulder, Colo.: Westview Press, 1994).

45. Ralph Lee Smith, *The Wired Nation: Cable TV, the Electronic Communications Highway* (New York: Harper and Row, 1972); Jennifer Light, *From Warfare to Welfare: Defense Intellectuals and Urban Problems in Cold War America* (Baltimore: Johns Hopkins University Press, 2003).

46. Megan Mullen, *The Rise of Cable Programming in the United States: Revolution or Evolution?* (Austin: University of Texas Press, 2003).

47. Frederick Wasser, *Veni, Vidi, Video: The Hollywood Empire and the VCR* (Austin: University of Texas Press, 2002); Joshua M. Greenberg, *From Betamax to Blockbuster: Video Stores and the Invention of Movies on Video* (Cambridge, Mass.: MIT Press, 2008).

48. William F. Baker and George Dessart, *Down the Tube: An Inside Account of the Failure of American Television* (New York: Basic Books, 1998).

49. Donna L. Halper, *Invisible Stars: A Social History of Women in American Broadcasting* (Armonk, N.Y.: M.E. Sharpe, 2001).

50. Tona J. Hangen, *Redeeming the Dial: Radio, Religion, and Popular Culture in America* (Chapel Hill: University of North Carolina Press, 2002).

51. Barbara Diane Savage, *Broadcasting Freedom: Radio, War, and the Politics of Race, 1938–1948* (Chapel Hill: University of North Carolina Press, 1999); Tim Brooks, *Lost Sounds: Blacks and the Birth of the Recording Industry, 1890–1919* (Champaign: University of Illinois Press, 2004); Clifford J. Doerksen, *American Babel: Rogue Radio Broadcasters of the Jazz Age* (Philadelphia: University of Pennsylvania Press, 2005).

52. Gregory J. Downey, *Closed Captioning: Subtitling, Stenography, and the Digital Convergence of Text with Television* (Baltimore: Johns Hopkins University Press, 2008).

Chapter 4

1. Kenneth Lipartito, "Picturephone and the Information Age: The Social Meaning of Failure," *Technology and Culture* 44 (2003): 50–81; William H. Dutton, Jay G. Blumler, and Kenneth L. Kraemer, eds., *Wired Cities: Shaping the Future of Communications* (Boston: Annenberg School of Communications, 1987).

2. Martin Campbell-Kelly and William Aspray, *Computer: A History of the Information Machine* (New York: Basic Books, 1996); Paul Ceruzzi, *A History of Modern Computing* (Cambridge, Mass.: MIT Press, 1998); Martin Campbell-Kelly, *From Airline Reservations to Sonic the Hedgehog: A History of the Software Industry* (Cambridge, Mass.: MIT Press, 2003).

3. Paul Edwards, *The Closed World: Computers and the Politics of Discourse in Cold War America* (Cambridge, Mass.: MIT Press, 1996).

4. Jennifer Light, "When Computers Were Women," *Technology and Culture* 40 (1999): 455–83.

5. Michael Riordan and Lillian Hoddeson, *Crystal Fire: The Birth of the Information Age* (New York: W.W. Norton, 1997).

6. Alfred D. Chandler Jr., *Inventing the Electronic Century: The Epic Story of the Consumer Electronics and Computer Industries* (Cambridge, Mass.: Harvard University Press, 2005).

7. James Cortada, *The Digital Hand*, vols. 1–3 (New York: Oxford University Press, 2004–08).

8. William Aspray, ed., *Computing before Computers* (Ames: Iowa State University Press, 1990).

9. JoAnne Yates, *Structuring the Information Age: Life Insurance and Technology in the Twentieth Century* (Baltimore: Johns Hopkins University Press, 2005).

10. Arthur L. Norberg and Judy E. O'Neill, *Transforming Computer Technology: Information Processing for the Pentagon, 1962–1986* (Baltimore: Johns Hopkins University Press, 1996).

11. Thomas P. Hughes, *Rescuing Prometheus* (New York: Pantheon Books, 1998).

12. Kent C. Redmond and Thomas M. Smith, *From Whirlwind to MITRE: The R&D Story of the SAGE Air Defense Computer* (Cambridge, Mass.: MIT Press, 2000).

13. Edwards, *The Closed World*.

14. Daniel Bell, *The Coming of the Post-Industrial Society: A Venture in Social Forecasting* (New York: Basic Books, 1973).

15. Nathan Ensmenger, *The Computer Boys Take Over: Computers, Programmers, and the Politics of Technical Expertise* (Cambridge, Mass.: MIT Press, 2010).

16. Thierry Bardini, *Bootstrapping: Douglas Engelbart, Coevolution, and the Origins of Personal Computing* (Stanford: Stanford University Press, 2000).

17. David Alan Grier, *When Computers Were Human* (Princeton: Princeton University Press, 2005).

18. Elizabeth F. Baker, *Displacement of Men by Machines: Effects of Technological Change in Commercial Printing* (New York: Columbia University Press, 1933).

19. David A. Mindell, *Between Human and Machine: Feedback, Control, and Computing before Cybernetics* (Baltimore: Johns Hopkins University Press, 2002).

20. Janet Abbate, *Inventing the Internet* (Cambridge, Mass.: MIT Press, 1999).

21. Fred Turner, *From Counterculture to Cyberculture: Stewart Brand, the Whole Earth Network, and the Rise of Digital Utopianism* (Chicago: University of Chicago Press, 2006).

22. Theodor H. Nelson, *Computer Lib/Dream Machines* (By the author, 1974), 5.

23. Stephen Kline, Nick Dyer-Witheford, and Greig de Peuter, *Digital Play: The Interaction of Technology, Culture, and Marketing* (Montréal: McGill-Queen's University Press, 2003).

24. Urs von Burg, *The Triumph of Ethernet: Technological Communities and the Battle for the LAN Standard* (Stanford: Stanford University Press, 2001).

25. Michael Benedikt, ed., *Cyberspace: First Steps* (Cambridge, Mass.: MIT Press, 1991); Rob Kitcin, *Cyberspace: The World in the Wires* (New York: John Wiley & Sons, 1998).

26. Tim Berners-Lee with Mark Fischetti, *Weaving the Web: The Original Design and Ultimate Destiny of the World Wide Web by Its Inventor* (San Francisco: HarperBusiness, 2000), 4.

27. James Gilles and Robert Cailliau, *How the Web Was Born: The Story of the World Wide Web* (Oxford: Oxford University Press, 2000).

28. Aharon Kellerman, *The Internet on Earth: A Geography of Information* (Hoboken, N.J.: John Wiley, 2002).

29. John Battelle, *The Search: How Google and Its Rivals Rewrote the Rules of Business and Transformed Our Culture* (New York: Portfolio, 2005).

30. Lawrence Lessig, *Code and Other Laws of Cyberspace* (New York: Basic Books, 1999), 6.

31. Greg Downey, "Virtual Webs, Physical Technologies, and Hidden Workers: The Spaces of Labor in Information Internetworks," *Technology and Culture* 42 (2001): 209–35; David Ellis, Rachel Oldridge, and Ana Vasconcelos, "Community and Virtual Community," *Annual Review of Information Science and Technology* 38 (2004): 145–86.

32. Barry Wellman, "Physical Place and Cyberplace: The Rise of Personalized Networking," *International Journal of Urban and Regional Research* 25 (2001): 227–52, quotation on 229.

33. Felix Stalder, *Manuel Castells: The Theory of the Network Society* (Malden, Mass.: Polity, 2006).

34. Manuel Castells, *The Informational City: Information Technology, Economic Restructuring, and the Urban-Regional Process* (New York: Blackwell, 1989), 348.

35. Manuel Castells, *The Information Age*, 3 vols. (Blackwell Publishers, 1996–98), vol. 1, *The Rise of the Network Society*, 412.

36. Matthew Zook, *The Geography of the Internet Industry* (New York: Blackwell, 2005).

37. Manuel Castells, ed., *The Network Society: A Cross-Cultural Perspective* (Northampton, Mass.: Edward Elgar, 2004).

38. Dan Schiller, *Digital Capitalism: Networking the Global Market System* (Cambridge, Mass.: MIT Press, 1999).

39. John Vernon Pavlik, *Journalism and New Media* (New York: Columbia University Press, 2001).

40. Pablo J. Boczkowski, *Digitizing the News: Innovation in Online Newspapers* (Cambridge, Mass.: MIT Press, 2004).

41. Jack Goldsmith and Tim Wu, *Who Controls the Internet? Illusions of a Borderless World* (New York: Oxford University Press, 2006).

42. Bill Gates, with Nathan Myhrvold and Peter Rinearson, *The Road Ahead* (New York: Viking, 1995); Esther Dyson, George Gilder, George Keyworth, and Alvin Toffler, "Cyberspace and the American Dream: A Magna Carta for the Knowledge Age," *The Information Society* 12 (1996): 295–308.

43. Langdon Winner, "Who Will We Be in Cyberspace?" *The Information Society* 12 (1996): 63–72.

44. Aad Blok and Greg Downey, eds., *Uncovering Labour in Information Revolutions, 1750–2000* (Cambridge: Cambridge University Press, 2003).

45. Greg Downey, "Commentary: The Place of Labor in the History of Information-Technology Revolutions," in *Uncovering Labour in Information Revolutions*, ed. Blok and Downey, 225–61.

46. Leah A. Lievrouw and Sharon E. Farb, "Information and Equity," *Annual Review of Information Science and Technology* 37 (2003): 499–540; Jan van Dijk and Kenneth Hacker, "The Digital Divide as a Complex and Dynamic Phenomenon," *The Information Society* 19 (2003): 315–26.

47. Pippa Norris, *Digital Divide: Civic Engagement, Information Poverty, and the Internet Worldwide* (Cambridge: Cambridge University Press, 2001), i.

48. Sherry Turkle, *Life on the Screen: Identity in the Age of the Internet* (New York: Simon & Schuster, 1995).

49. Marc A. Smith and Peter Kollock, eds., *Communities in Cyberspace* (New York: Routledge, 1999); Beth E. Kolko, Lisa Nakamura, and Gilbert B. Rodman, eds., *Race in Cyberspace* (New York: Routledge, 2000); Lisa Nakamura, *Cybertypes: Race, Ethnicity, and Identity on the Internet* (New York: Routledge, 2002); Karen E. Riggs, *Granny @ Work: Aging and New Technology on the Job in America* (New York: Routledge, 2004).

CONCLUSION

1. Todd Gitlin, *Media Unlimited: How the Torrent of Images and Sounds Overwhelms our Lives* (New York: Henry Holt and Co., 2002), 17.

2. Barbie Zelizer and Stuart Allan, eds., *Journalism after September 11* (New York: Routledge, 2002).

3. Stuart Allan, "Reweaving the Internet: Online News of September 11," in *Journalism after September 11*, ed. Zelizer and Allan, 119–40.

4. James W. Carey, "American Journalism On, Before, and After September 11," in *Journalism after September 11*, ed. Zelizer and Allan, 71–90, quotation on 76.

5. Susan J. Douglas, "The Turn Within: The Irony of Technology in a Globalized World," *American Quarterly* 57 (2006): 619–38, quotation on 617.

6. Robert W. McChesney, *Rich Media, Poor Democracy* (New York: New Press, 2000), 60.

7. Sheldon Rampton and John Stauber, *Weapons of Mass Deception: The Uses of Propaganda in Bush's War on Iraq* (New York: Penguin, 2003).

8. Neil Postman, *Amusing Ourselves to Death: Public Discourse in the Age of Show Business* (New York: Penguin Books, 1985), 16.

9. Tim O'Reilly, "What is Web 2.0? Design Patterns and Business Models for the Next Generation of Software," September 30, 2005, http://oreilly.com/web2/archive/what-is-web-20.html.

BIBLIOGRAPHY

Abbate, Janet. *Inventing the Internet.* Cambridge, Mass., MIT Press, 1999.

Acland, Charles R., ed. *Residual Media.* Minneapolis: University of Minnesota Press, 2007.

Allan, Stuart. "Reweaving the Internet: Online News of September 11." In *Journalism after September 11,* edited by Barbie Zelizer and Stuart Allan. New York: Routledge, 2002.

Amory, Hugh, and David D. Hall, eds. *A History of the Book in America.* 5 vols. Vol. 1, Cambridge: Cambridge University Press, 1999; Vols. 2–5, Chapel Hill: University of North Carolina Press, 2006–10.

Anderson, Benedict. *Imagined Communities: Reflections on the Origin and Spread of Nationalism.* London: Verso, 1983.

Anderson, Margo J. *The American Census: A Social History.* New Haven, Conn.: Yale University Press, 1988.

Ang, Ien. "The Nature of the Audience." In *Questioning the Media: A Critical Introduction,* edited by John Downing, Ali Mohammadi, and Annabelle Sreberny-Mohammadi. 2d ed. Thousand Oaks, Calif: SAGE, 1995.

Aspray, William, ed. *Computing before Computers.* Ames: Iowa State University, 1990.

Augst, Thomas, and Kenneth Carpenter, eds. *Institutions of Reading: The Social Life of Libraries in the United States.* Amherst: University of Massachusetts Press, 2007.

Bagdikian, Ben. *The New Media Monopoly.* Boston: Beacon Press, 2004.

Baker, Elizabeth F. *Displacement of Men by Machines: Effects of Technological Change in Commercial Printing.* New York: Columbia University Press, 1933.

Baker, William F., and George Dessart. *Down the Tube: An Inside Account of the Failure of American Television.* New York: Basic Books, 1998.

Baldasty, Gerald J. "The Rise of News as a Commodity: Business Imperatives and the Press in the Nineteenth Century." In *Ruthless Criticism: New Perspectives in U.S. Communication History,* edited by William S. Solomon and Robert W. McChesney. Minneapolis: University of Minnes, ota Press, 1993.

Baldwin, Neil. *Edison: Inventing the Century.* New York: Hyperion, 1995.

Bardini, Thierry. *Bootstrapping: Douglas Engelbart, Coevolution, and the Origins of Personal Computing.* Stanford: Stanford University Press, 2000.

Barnouw, Erik. *Tube of Plenty: The Evolution of American Television.* 2d ed. New York: Oxford University Press, 1990.

Battelle, John. *The Search: How Google and Its Rivals Rewrote the Rules of Business and Transformed Our Culture.* New York: Portfolio, 2005.

Baughman, James L. *The Republic of Mass Culture: Journalism, Filmmaking, and Broadcasting in America since 1941.* Baltimore: Johns Hopkins University Press, 2006.

Beales, Ross W., and E. Jennifer Monaghan. "Literacy and Schoolbooks." In *A History of the Book in America,* vol. 1: *The Colonial Book in the Atlantic World,* Hugh Amory and David D. Hall, eds. vol. 1. Chapel Hill: University of North Carolina Press, 2007.

Bell, Daniel. *The Coming of the Post-Industrial Society: A Venture in Social Forecasting.* New York: Basic Books, 1973.

Benedikt, Michael, ed. *Cyberspace: First Steps.* Cambridge, Mass.: MIT Press, 1991.

Beniger, James R. *The Control Revolution: Technological and Economic Origins of the Information Society.* Cambridge, Mass.: Harvard University Press, 1986.

Bernays, Edward L. *Propaganda.* New York: H. Liveright, 1928.

Berners-Lee, Tim, with Mark Fischetti. *Weaving the Web: The Original Design and Ultimate Destiny of the World Wide Web by its Inventor.* San Francisco: HarperBusiness, 2000.

Bijker, Wiebe E., Thomas Parke Hughes, and Trevor J. Pinch, eds. *The Social Construction of Technological Systems: New Directions in the Sociology and History of Technology.* Cambridge, Mass.: MIT Press, 1987.

Bix, Amy Sue. *Inventing Ourselves out of Jobs? America's Debate over Technological Unemployment, 1929–1981.* Baltimore: Johns Hopkins University Press, 2000.

Blakely, Robert J. *To Serve the Public Interest: Educational Broadcasting in the United States.* Syracuse: Syracuse University Press, 1979.

Blok, Aad, and Greg Downey, eds. *Uncovering Labour in Information Revolutions, 1750–2000.* Cambridge: Cambridge University Press, 2003.

Blondheim, Menahem. *News over the Wires: The Telegraph and the Flow of Public Information in America, 1844–1897.* Cambridge, Mass.: Harvard University Press, 1994.

Bloom, Jonathan M. *Paper before Print: The History and Impact of Paper in the Islamic World.* New Haven, Conn.: Yale University Press, 2001.

Boczkowski, Pablo J. *Digitizing the News: Innovation in Online Newspapers.* Cambridge, Mass.: MIT Press, 2004.

Boddy, William. "Television Begins." In *Television: An International History*, edited by Anthony Smith. New York: Oxford University Press, 1995.

Bowker, Geoffrey C., and Susan Leigh Star. *Sorting Things Out: Classification and Its Consequences.* Cambridge, Mass.: MIT Press, 1999.

Brandt, Deborah. *Literacy in American Lives.* New York: Cambridge University Press, 2001.

Braun, Hans-Joachim, ed. *Music and Technology in the 20th Century.* Baltimore: Johns Hopkins University Press, 2002.

Braverman, Harry. *Labor and Monopoly Capital: The Degradation of Work in the Twentieth Century.* New York: Monthly Review Press, 1974.

Brock, Gerald W. *The Second Information Revolution.* Cambridge, Mass.: Harvard University Press, 2003.

———. *The Telecommunications Industry: The Dynamics of Market Structure.* Cambridge, Mass.: Harvard University Press, 1981.

Brooks, Tim. *Lost Sounds: Blacks and the Birth of the Recording Industry, 1890–1919.* Champaign: University of Illinois Press, 2004.

Brown, Candy Gunther. *The Word in the World: Evangelical Writing, Publishing, and Reading in America, 1789–1880.* Chapel Hill: University of North Carolina Press, 2004.

Brown, Joshua. *Beyond the Lines: Pictorial Reporting, Everyday Life, and the Crisis of Gilded Age America.* Berkeley: University of California Press, 2002.

Brown, Richard D. "Early American Origins of the Information Age." In *A Nation Transformed by Information: How Information Has Shaped the United States from Colonial Times to the Present*, edited by Alfred D. Chandler Jr. and James W. Cortada. New York: Oxford University Press, 2000.

———. *Knowledge is Power: The Diffusion of Information in Early America, 1700–1865.* New York: Oxford University Press, 1989.

Butsch, Richard. *The Making of American Audiences: From Stage to Television, 1750–1990.* New York: Cambridge University Press, 2000.

Cairncross, Frances. *The Death of Distance: How the Communications Revolution Is Changing our Lives.* Cambridge, Mass.: Harvard Business School Press, 1997.

Campbell-Kelly, Martin. *From Airline Reservations to Sonic the Hedgehog: A History of the Software Industry.* Cambridge, Mass.: MIT Press, 2003.

Campbell-Kelly, Martin, and William Aspray. *Computer: A History of the Information Machine.* New York: Basic Books, 1996.

Carey, James W. "American Journalism On, Before, and After September 11." In *Journalism after September 11*, edited by Barbie Zelizer and Stuart Allan. New York: Routledge, 2002.

Carnegie Commission on Educational Television. *Public Television: A Program for Action*. New York: Bantam, 1967.

Castells, Manuel. *The Information Age*, 3 vols. New York: Blackwell, 1996–98.

———. *The Informational City: Information Technology, Economic Restructuring, and the Urban-Regional Process*. New York: Blackwell, 1989.

———, ed. *The Network Society: A Cross-Cultural Perspective*. Northampton, Mass.: Edward Elgar, 2004.

Castells, Manuel, Mireia Fernandez-Ardevol, Jack Linchuan Qiu, and Araba Sey. *Mobile Communication and Society: A Global Perspective*. Cambridge, Mass.: MIT Press, 2006.

Ceruzzi, Paul. *A History of Modern Computing*. Cambridge, Mass.: MIT Press, 1998.

Chandler, Alfred D., Jr. *Inventing the Electronic Century: The Epic Story of the Consumer Electronics and Computer Industries*. Cambridge, Mass.: Harvard University Press, 2005.

———. *The Visible Hand: The Managerial Revolution in American Business*. Cambridge, Mass.: Belknap Press, 1977.

Chandler, Alfred D., Jr., and James W. Cortada, eds. *A Nation Transformed by Information: How Information Has Shaped the United States from Colonial Times to the Present*. New York: Oxford University Press, 2000.

Clarke, Richard A., and Robert K. Knake. *Cyber War: The Next Threat to National Security and What to Do about It*. New York: HarperCollins, 2010.

Cortada, James. *The Digital Hand*. Vols. 1–3. New York: Oxford University Press, 2004–08.

Cowan, Ruth Schwartz. *More Work for Mother: The Ironies of Household Technology from the Open Hearth to the Microwave*. New York: Basic Books, 1983.

———. *A Social History of American Technology*. New York: Oxford University Press, 1997.

Crafton, Donald. *The Talkies: American Cinema's Transition to Sound, 1926–1931*. New York: Scribner, 1997.

Craig, Douglas. *Fireside Politics: Radio and Political Culture in the United States, 1920–1940*. Baltimore: Johns Hopkins University Press, 2000.

Cronon, William. *Nature's Metropolis: Chicago and the Great West*. New York: W.W. Norton & Co., 1991.

Czitrom, Daniel. *Media and the American Mind: From Morse to McLuhan.* Chapel Hill: University of North Carolina Press, 1982.

Danky, James P., and Wayne A. Wiegand, eds. *Print Culture in a Diverse America.* Urbana: University of Illinois Press, 1998.

Davies, Margery. *Woman's Place Is at the Typewriter: Office Work and Office Workers, 1870–1930.* Philadelphia: Temple University Press, 1982.

Denning, Michael. *Mechanic Accents: Dime Novels and Working-Class Culture in America.* Rev. ed. New York: Verso, 1998.

Doerksen, Clifford J. *American Babel: Rogue Radio Broadcasters of the Jazz Age.* Philadelphia: University of Pennsylvania Press, 2005.

Douglas, Susan J. *Inventing American Broadcasting, 1899–1922.* Baltimore: Johns Hopkins University Press, 1987.

———. *Listening In: Radio and the American Imagination, from Amos 'n' Andy and Edward R. Murrow to Wolfman Jack and Howard Stern.* New York: Times Books, 1999.

———. "The Turn Within: The Irony of Technology in a Globalized World." *American Quarterly* 57 (2006): 619–38.

Downey, Greg. *Closed Captioning: Subtitling, Stenography, and the Digital Convergence of Text with Television.* Baltimore: Johns Hopkins University Press, 2008.

———. "Commentary: The Place of Labor in the History of Information-Technology Revolutions." In *Uncovering Labour in Information Revolutions, 1750–2000,* edited by Aad Blok and Greg Downey. Cambridge: Cambridge University Press, 2003.

———. *Telegraph Messenger Boys: Labor, Technology, and Geography, 1850–1950.* New York: Routledge, 2002.

———. "Virtual Webs, Physical Technologies, and Hidden Workers: The Spaces of Labor in Information Internetworks." *Technology and Culture* 42 (2001): 209–35.

Downing, John, Ali Mohammadi, and Annabelle Sreberny-Mohammadi, eds. *Questioning the Media: A Critical Introduction.* 2d ed. Thousand Oaks, Calif.: SAGE, 1995.

Dutton, William H., Jay G. Blumler, and Kenneth L. Kraemer, eds. *Wired Cities: Shaping the Future of Communications.* Boston: Annenberg School of Communications, 1987.

Dyer, Richard. "Making 'White' People White." In *The Social Shaping of Technology,* edited by Donald MacKenzie and Judy Wajcman. 2d ed. Philadelphia: Open University Press, 1999.

Dyson, Esther, George Gilder, George Keyworth, and Alvin Toffler. "Cyberspace and the American Dream: A Magna Carta for the Knowledge Age." *The Information Society* 12 (1996): 295–308.

Edgerton, David. "Innovation, Technology, and History: What is the Historiography of Technology About?" *Technology and Culture* 51 (2010): 680–97.

———. *The Shock of the Old: Technology and Global History since 1900.* New York: Oxford, 2007.

Edwards, Paul. *The Closed World: Computers and the Politics of Discourse in Cold War America.* Cambridge, Mass.: MIT Press, 1996.

———. "Infrastructure and Modernity: Force, Time, and Social Organization in the History of Sociotechnical Systems." In *Modernity and Technology*, edited by Thomas J. Misa, Philip Brey, and Andrew Feenberg. Cambridge, Mass.: MIT Press, 2003.

———. "Y2K: Millennial Reflections on Computers as Infrastructure." *History and Technology* 15 (1998): 7–29.

Eisenstein, Elizabeth. *The Printing Press as an Agent of Change: Communications and Cultural Transformations in Early Modern Europe*, 2 vols. New York: Cambridge University Press, 1979.

Ellis, David. Rachel Oldridge, and Ana Vasconcelos. "Community and Virtual Community." *Annual Review of Information Science and Technology* 38 (2004): 145–86.

Ensmenger, Nathan. *The Computer Boys Take Over: Computers, Programmers, and the Politics of Technical Expertise.* Cambridge, Mass.: MIT Press, 2010.

Ewen, Stuart. *Captains of Consciousness: Advertising and the Social Roots of Consumer Culture.* New York: McGraw-Hill, 1976.

Fields, Gary. *Territories of Profit: Communications, Capitalist Development, and the Innovative Enterprises of G. F. Swift and Dell Computer.* Stanford: Stanford University Press, 2003.

Fischer, Claude S. *America Calling: A Social History of the Telephone to 1940.* Berkeley: University of California Press, 1992.

Fuller, Wayne E. *Morality and the Mail in Nineteenth-Century America.* Champaign: University of Illinois Press, 2003.

Füssel, Stephan. *Gutenberg and the Impact of Printing.* Burlington, Vt.: Ashgate, 2005.

Gabler, Edwin. *The American Telegrapher: A Social History, 1860–1900.* New Brunswick: Rutgers University Press, 1988.

Gandy, Oscar H., Jr. "Tracking the Audience: Personal Information and Privacy." In *Questioning the Media: A Critical Introduction*, edited by John Downing, Ali Mohammadi, and Annabelle Sreberny-Mohammadi. 2d ed. Thousand Oaks, Calif.: SAGE, 1995.

Garrison, Dee. *Apostles of Culture: The Public Librarian and American Society, 1876–1920.* New York: Free Press, 1979.

Gates, Bill, with Nathan Myhrvold and Peter Rinearson. *The Road Ahead.* New York: Viking, 1995.

Gilles, James, and Robert Cailliau. *How the Web Was Born: The Story of the World Wide Web.* Oxford: Oxford University Press, 2000.

Gillespie, Tarleton. *Wired Shut: Copyright and the Shape of Digital Culture.* Cambridge, Mass.: MIT Press, 2007.

Gitelman, Lisa. *Always Already New: New Media, History, and the Data of Culture.* Cambridge, Mass.: MIT Press, 2006.

Gitlin, Todd. *Media Unlimited: How the Torrent of Images and Sounds Overwhelms Our Lives.* New York: Henry Holt and Co., 2002.

Goldsmith Jack, and Tim Wu. *Who Controls the Internet? Illusions of a Borderless World.* New York: Oxford University Press, 2006.

Gomery, Douglas. *The Coming of Sound: A History.* New York: Routledge, 2005.

———. *Shared Pleasures: A History of Movie Presentation in the United States.* Madison: University of Wisconsin Press, 1992.

Goody, Jack. *The Interface between the Written and the Oral.* New York: Cambridge University Press, 1987.

Graff, Harvey. *The Legacies of Literacy: Continuities and Contradictions in Western Culture and Society.* Bloomington: Indiana University Press, 1991.

Graham, Margaret. "The Threshold of the Information Age: Radio, Television, and Motion Pictures Mobilize the Nation." In *A Nation Transformed by Information: How Information Has Shaped the United States from Colonial Times to the Present,* edited by Alfred D. Chandler Jr. and James W. Cortada. New York: Oxford University Press, 2000.

Graham, Stephen, and Simon Marvin. *Splintering Urbanism: Networked Infrastructures, Technological Mobilities and the Urban Condition.* New York: Routledge, 2001.

———. *Telecommunications and the City: Electronic Spaces, Urban Places.* New York: Routledge, 1996.

Green, Venus. *Race on the Line: Gender, Labor, and Technology in the Bell System, 1880–1980.* Durham, N.C.: Duke University Press, 2001.

Greenberg, Joshua M. *From Betamax to Blockbuster: Video Stores and the Invention of Movies on Video.* Cambridge, Mass.: MIT Press, 2008.

Grier, David Alan. *When Computers Were Human.* Princeton, N.J.: Princeton University Press, 2005.

Gudis, Catherine. *Buyways: Billboards, Automobiles, and the American Landscape.* New York: Routledge, 2003.

Habermas, Jürgen. *The Structural Transformation of the Public Sphere: An Inquiry into a Category of Bourgeois Society.* Cambridge, Mass.: MIT Press, 1989.

Halper, Donna L. *Invisible Stars: A Social History of Women in American Broadcasting.* Armonk, N.Y.: M.E. Sharpe, 2001.

Hangen, Tona J. *Redeeming the Dial: Radio, Religion, and Popular Culture in America.* Chapel Hill: University of North Carolina Press, 2002.

Haring, Kristen. *Ham Radio's Technical Culture.* Cambridge, Mass: MIT Press, 2007.

Harvey, David. *The Condition of Postmodernity: An Enquiry into the Origins of Cultural Change.* Cambridge, Mass.: Blackwell, 1989.

Henkin, David M. *City Reading: Written Words and Public Spaces in Antebellum New York.* New York: Columbia University Press, 1998.

———. *The Postal Age: The Emergence of Modern Communications in Nineteenth-Century America.* Chicago: University of Chicago Press, 2006.

Hepworth, Mark E. *Geography of the Information Economy.* New York: The Guilford Press, 1990.

Herman, Edward S., and Robert W. McChesney. *The Global Media: The New Missionaries of Corporate Capitalism.* London: Cassell, 1997.

Hoynes, William. *Public Television For Sale: Media, the Market, and the Public Sphere.* Boulder, Colo.: Westview Press, 1994.

Hughes, Thomas P. *American Genesis: A Century of Invention and Technological Enthusiasm, 1870–1970.* New York: Viking, 1989.

———. *Networks of Power: Electrification in Western Society, 1880–1930.* Baltimore: Johns Hopkins University Press, 1985.

———. *Rescuing Prometheus.* New York: Pantheon Books, 1998.

Israel, Paul. *Edison: A Life of Invention.* New York: John Wiley and Sons, 1998.

———. *From Machine Shop to Industrial Laboratory: Telegraphy and the Changing Context of American Invention, 1830–1920.* Baltimore: Johns Hopkins University Press, 1992.

Janelle, Donald G. "Global Interdependence and its Consequences." In *Collapsing Space and Time: Geographic Aspects of Communication and Information,* edited by Stanley D. Brunn and Thomas R. Leinbach. London: HarperCollins Academic, 1991.

Jenkins, Reese V. *Images and Enterprise: Technology and the American Photographic Industry, 1839 to 1925.* Baltimore: Johns Hopkins University Press, 1975.

————. "Technology and the Market: George Eastman and the Origins of Mass Amateur Photography." In *Technology and American History: A Historical Anthology*, edited by Stephen H. Cutcliffe and Terry S. Reynolds. Chicago: University of Chicago Press, 1997.

————. "Words, Images, Artifacts and Sound: Documents for the History of Technology." *British Journal of the History of Science* 20 (1987): 39–56.

Jepsen, Thomas C. *My Sisters Telegraphic: Women in the Telegraph Office, 1846–1950*. Athens: Ohio University Press, 2000.

John, Richard R. *Network Nation: Inventing American Telecommunications*. Cambridge, Mass.: Belknap Press, 2010.

————. "Recasting the Information Infrastructure for the Industrial Age." In *A Nation Transformed by Information: How Information Has Shaped the United States from Colonial Times to the Present*, edited by Alfred D. Chandler Jr. and James W. Cortada. New York: Oxford University Press, 2000.

————. *Spreading the News: The American Postal System from Franklin to Morse*. Cambridge, Mass.: Harvard University Press, 1995.

Johns, Adrian. *The Nature of the Book: Print and Knowledge in the Making*. Chicago: University of Chicago Press, 1998.

Kanigel, Robert. *The One Best Way: Frederick Winslow Taylor and the Enigma of Efficiency*. New York: Viking, 1997.

Kellerman, Aharon. *The Internet on Earth: A Geography of Information*. Hoboken, N.J.: John Wiley, 2002.

————. *Telecommunications and Geography*. London: Belhaven 1993.

Kern, Stephen. *The Culture of Time and Space, 1880–1918*. Cambridge, Mass.: Harvard University Press, 1983.

Kitch, Carolyn. *The Girl on the Magazine Cover: The Origins of Visual Stereotypes in American Mass Media*. Chapel Hill: University of North Carolina Press, 2001.

Kitchin, Rob. *Cyberspace: The World in the Wires*. New York: John Wiley & Sons, 1998.

Kline, Stephen, Nick Dyer-Witheford, and Greig de Peuter. *Digital Play: The Interaction of Technology, Culture, and Marketing*. Montréal: McGill-Queen's University Press, 2003.

Kolko, Beth E., Lisa Nakamura, and Gilbert B. Rodman, eds. *Race in Cyberspace*. New York: Routledge, 2000.

Kraft, James P. *Stage to Studio: Musicians and the Sound Revolution, 1890–1950*. Baltimore: Johns Hopkins University Press, 1996.

Laird, Pamela Walker. *Advertising Progress: American Business and the Rise of Consumer Marketing*. Baltimore: Johns Hopkins University Press, 1998.

Larson, John Lauritz. *Internal Improvement: National Public Works and the Promise of Popular Government in the Early United States.* Chapel Hill: University of North Carolina, 2001.

Lasswell, Harold D. "The Structure and Function of Communication in Society." In *The Communication of Ideas,* edited by Lyman Bryson. New York: Cooper Square, 1964.

Lears, Jackson. *Fables of Abundance: A Cultural History of Advertising in America.* New York: Basic Books, 1994.

Lehuu, Isabelle. *Carnival on the Page: Popular Print Media in Antebellum America.* Chapel Hill: University of North Carolina Press, 2000.

Lenert, Edward M. "A Communication Theory Perspective on Telecommunications Policy." *Journal of Communication* 48 (1998): 3–23.

Lessig, Lawrence. *Code and Other Laws of Cyberspace.* New York: Basic Books, 1999.

Lievrouw, Leah A., and Sharon E. Farb. "Information and Equity." *Annual Review of Information Science and Technology* 37 (2003): 499–540.

Light, Jennifer. *From Warfare to Welfare: Defense Intellectuals and Urban Problems in Cold War America.* Baltimore: Johns Hopkins University Press, 2003.

———. "When Computers Were Women." *Technology and Culture* 40 (1999): 455–83.

Lipartito, Kenneth. "Picturephone and the Information Age: The Social Meaning of Failure." *Technology and Culture* 44 (2003): 50–81.

Lippmann, Walter. *Public Opinion.* New York: Harcourt Brace, 1922.

Lubar, Stephen. *Infoculture: The Smithsonian Book of Information Age Inventions.* Boston: Houghton Mifflin, 1993.

MacDougall, Robert. "The People's Telephone: The Politics of Telephony in the United States and Canada." *Enterprise and Society* 6 (2005): 581–87.

———. "The Wire Devils: Pulp Thrillers, the Telephone, and Action at a Distance in the Wiring of a Nation." *American Quarterly* 57 (2006): 715–41.

MacKenzie, Donald, and Judy Wajcman, eds. *The Social Shaping of Technology.* 2d ed. Philadelphia: Open University Press, 1999.

Magee, Gary Bryan. *Productivity and Performance in the Paper Industry: Labour, Capital, and Technology in Britain and America, 1860–1914.* Cambridge: Cambridge University Press, 1997.

Marien, Mary Warner. *Photography and Its Critics: A Cultural History, 1839–1900.* Cambridge: Cambridge University Press, 1998.

Marvin, Carolyn. *When Old Technologies Were New: Thinking about Electric Communication in the Late Nineteenth Century.* New York: Oxford University Press, 1988.

McChesney, Robert W. *Rich Media, Poor Democracy*. New York: New Press, 2000.

McGaw, Judith A. *Most Wonderful Machine: Mechanization and Social Change in Berkshire Paper Making, 1801–1885*. Princeton, N.J.: Princeton University Press, 1987.

McHenry, Elizabeth. *Forgotten Readers: Recovering the Lost History of African American Literary Societies*. Durham: Duke University Press, 2002.

McLuhan, Marshall. *Understanding Media: The Extensions of Man*. New York: New American Library, 1964.

Meyrowitz, Joshua. *No Sense of Place: The Impact of Electronic Media on Social Behavior*. New York: Oxford University Press, 1985.

Mindell, David A. *Between Human and Machine: Feedback, Control, and Computing before Cybernetics*. Baltimore: Johns Hopkins University Press, 2002.

Mitchell, William. *City of Bits: Space, Place, and the Infobahn*. Cambridge, Mass.: MIT Press, 1995.

Montgomery, David. *Workers' Control in America: Studies in the History of Work, Technology, and Labor Struggles*. New York: Cambridge University Press, 1979.

Morton, David. *Off the Record: The Technology and Culture of Sound Recording in America*. New Brunswick: Rutgers University Press, 2000.

Mueller, Milton L., Jr. *Universal Service: Competition, Interconnection, and Monopoly in the Making of the American Telephone System*. Cambridge, Mass.: MIT Press, 1997.

Mullen, Megan. *The Rise of Cable Programming in the United States: Revolution or Evolution?* Austin: University of Texas Press, 2003.

Murray, James B., Jr. *Wireless Nation: The Frenzied Launch of the Cellular Revolution in America*. Cambridge, Mass.: Perseus, 2001.

Nachman, Gerald. *Raised on Radio*. New York: Pantheon Books, 1998.

Nakamura, Lisa. *Cybertypes: Race, Ethnicity, and Identity on the Internet*. New York: Routledge, 2002.

Nasaw, David. *Children of the City: At Work and At Play*. New York: Oxford University Press 1985.

Negroponte, Nicholas. *Being Digital*. New York: Knopf, 1995.

Nelson, Theodor H. *Computer Lib/Dream Machines*. By the author, 1974.

Newman, Kathy. *Radio Active: Advertising and Consumer Activism, 1935–1947*. Berkeley: University of California Press, 2004.

Norberg, Arthur L., and Judy E. O'Neill. *Transforming Computer Technology: Information Processing for the Pentagon, 1962–1986*. Baltimore: Johns Hopkins University Press, 1996.

Nord, David Paul. *Communities of Journalism: A History of American Newspapers and their Readers.* Urbana: University of Illinois Press, 2001.

Norris, Pippa. *Digital Divide: Civic Engagement, Information Poverty, and the Internet Worldwide.* Cambridge: Cambridge University Press, 2001.

Olivier, Marc. "George Eastman's Modern Stone-Age Family: Snapshot Photography and the Brownie." *Technology and Culture* 48 (2007): 1–19.

Olson, David R., and Michael Cole, eds. *Technology, Literacy, and the Evolution of Society: Implications of the Work of Jack Goody.* Mahwah, N.J.: Lawrence Erlbaum, 2006.

Ong, Walter J., S.J. *Orality and Literacy: The Technologizing of the Word.* New York: Methuen, 1982.

Ostrowski, Carl. *Books, Maps, and Politics: A Cultural History of the Library of Congress, 1783–1861.* Amherst: University of Massachusetts Press, 2004.

Panzer, Mary. *Mathew Brady and the Image of History.* Washington, D.C.: Smithsonian Books, 1997.

Pavlik, John Vernon. *Journalism and New Media.* New York: Columbia University Press, 2001.

Post, Robert C. *Technology, Transport, and Travel in American History.* Washington D.C.: Society for the History of Technology/American Historical Association, 2003.

Postman, Neil. *Amusing Ourselves to Death: Public Discourse in the Age of Show Business.* New York: Penguin Books, 1985.

Pred, Allan R. *Urban Growth and the Circulation of Information: The United States System of Cities, 1790–1840.* Cambridge, Mass.: Harvard University Press, 1973.

Pursell, Carroll, ed. *A Companion to American Technology.* Malden, Mass.: Blackwell, 2005.

Rampton, Sheldon, and John Stauber. *Weapons of Mass Deception: The Uses of Propaganda in Bush's War on Iraq.* New York: Penguin, 2003.

Raven, James. *London Booksellers and American Customers: Transatlantic Literary Community and the Charleston Library Society, 1748–1811.* Columbia: University of South Carolina Press, 2002.

Redmond, Kent C., and Thomas M. Smith. *From Whirlwind to MITRE: The R&D Story of the SAGE Air Defense Computer.* Cambridge, Mass.: MIT Press, 2000.

Remer, Rosalind. *Printers and Men of Capital: Philadelphia Book Publishers in the New Republic.* Philadelphia: University of Pennsylvania Press, 1996.

Riggs, Karen E. *Granny @ Work: Aging and New Technology on the Job in America.* New York: Routledge, 2004.

Riis, Jacob A. *How the Other Half Lives: Studies Among the Tenements of New York.* Boston: Bedford Books, 1996.

Riordan, Michael, and Lillian Hoddeson. *Crystal Fire: The Birth of the Information Age.* New York: W. W. Norton, 1997.

Roland, Alex. *Strategic Computing: DARPA and the Quest for Machine Intelligence, 1983–1993.* Cambridge, Mass: MIT Press, 2002.

Rumble, Walker. *The Swifts: Printers in the Age of Typesetting Races.* Charlottesville: University of Virginia Press, 2003.

Saenger, Paul. *Space between Words: The Origins of Silent Reading.* Stanford: Stanford University Press, 1997.

Sassen, Saskia. *Cities in a World Economy.* Thousand Oaks, Calif.: Pine Forge Press, 1994.

Savage, Barbara Diane. *Broadcasting Freedom: Radio, War, and the Politics of Race, 1938–1948.* Chapel Hill: University of North Carolina, 1999.

Schiller, Dan. *Digital Capitalism: Networking the Global Market System.* Cambridge, Mass.: MIT Press, 1999.

———. *Theorizing Communication: A History.* New York: Oxford University Press, 1996.

Schudson, Michael. *Discovering the News: A Social History of American Newspapers.* New York: Basic Books, 1978.

———. "News, Public, Nation." *American Historical Review* 107 (2002): 481–95.

Schultz, James. *The Romance of Small-Town Chautauquas.* Columbia: University of Missouri Press, 2002.

Sharpe, Kevin, and Steven N. Zwicker, eds. *Reading, Society and Politics in Early Modern England.* New York: Cambridge University Press, 2003.

Sklar, Robert. *Movie-made America: A Cultural History of American Movies.* 2d ed. New York: Vintage, 1994.

Slotten, Hugh R. *Radio and Television Regulation: Broadcast Technology in the United States, 1920–1960.* Baltimore: Johns Hopkins University Press, 2000.

Smith, Marc A., and Peter Kollock, eds. *Communities in Cyberspace.* New York: Routledge, 1999.

Smith, Merritt Roe, and Leo Marx, eds. *Does Technology Drive History? The Dilemma of Technological Determinism.* Cambridge, Mass.: MIT Press, 1994.

Smith, Ralph Lee. *The Wired Nation: Cable TV, the Electronic Communications Highway.* New York: Harper and Row, 1972.

Smythe, Dallas. *Dependency Road: Communications, Capitalism, Consciousness, and Canada.* Norwood, N. J.: Ablex, 1981.

Solomon, William S., and Robert W. McChesney, eds. *Ruthless Criticism: New Perspectives in U.S. Communication History.* Minneapolis: University of Minnesota Press, 1993.

Spigel, Lynn. *Make Room for TV: Television and the Family Ideal in Postwar America.* Chicago: University of Chicago Press, 1992.

Stalder, Felix. *Manuel Castells: The Theory of the Network Society.* Malden, Mass.: Polity, 2006.

Standage, Tom. *The Victorian Internet: The Remarkable Story of the Telegraph and the Nineteenth Century's On-Line Pioneers.* New York: Walker and Company, 1998.

Starr, Paul. *The Creation of the Media: Political Origins of Modern Communications.* New York: Basic Books, 2004.

Sterne, Jonathan. *The Audible Past: Cultural Origins of Sound Reproduction.* Durham, N.C.: Duke University Press, 2003.

Tarr, Joel A., with Thomas Finholt and David Goodman. "The City and the Telegraph: Urban Telecommunications in the Pre-Telephone Era." *Journal of Urban History* 14 (1987): 38–80.

Taylor, Frederick Winslow. *The Principles of Scientific Management.* New York: Harper & Brothers, 1911.

Taylor, Timothy D. *Strange Sounds: Music, Technology, & Culture.* New York: Routledge, 2001.

Thompson, Emily. *The Soundscape of Modernity: Architectural Acoustics and the Culture of Listening in America, 1900–1933.* Cambridge, Mass.: MIT Press, 2002.

Thornton, Tamara Plakins. *Handwriting in America: A Cultural History.* New Haven, Conn.: Yale University Press, 1996.

Toffler, Alvin. *The Third Wave.* New York: Morrow, 1980.

Turkle, Sherry. *Life on the Screen: Identity in the Age of the Internet.* New York: Simon & Schuster, 1995.

Turner, Fred. *From Counterculture to Cyberculture: Stewart Brand, the Whole Earth Network, and the Rise of Digital Utopianism.* Chicago: University of Chicago Press, 2006.

Turow, Joseph. *Breaking Up America: Advertisers and the New Media World.* Chicago: University of Chicago Press, 1997.

Twitchell, James B. *Adcult USA: The Triumph of Advertising in American Culture.* New York: Columbia University Press, 1996.

Vaidhyanathan, Siva. *Copyrights and Copywrongs: The Rise of Intellectual Property and How it Threatens Creativity*. New York: New York University Press, 2001.

van Dijk, Jan, and Kenneth Hacker. "The Digital Divide as a Complex and Dynamic Phenomenon." *The Information Society* 19 (2003): 315–26.

von Burg, Urs. *The Triumph of Ethernet: Technological Communities and the Battle for the LAN Standard*. Stanford, Calif.: Stanford University Press, 2001.

Wallace, Aurora. *Newspapers and the Making of Modern America: A History*. Westport, Conn.: Greenwood Press, 2005.

Wasser, Frederick. *Veni, Vidi, Video: The Hollywood Empire and the VCR*. Austin: University of Texas Press, 2002.

Weinstein, David. *The Forgotten Network: DuMont and the Birth of American Television*. Philadelphia: Temple University Press, 2004.

Wellman, Barry. "Physical Place and Cyberplace: The Rise of Personalized Networking." *International Journal of Urban and Regional Research* 25 (2001): 227–52.

Wheeler, James O., Yuko Aoyama and Barney Warf, eds. *Cities in the Telecommunications Age: The Fracturing of Geographies*. New York: Routledge, 2000.

Wheeler, Tom. *Mr. Lincoln's T-Mails: The Untold Story of How Abraham Lincoln Used the Telegraph to Win the Civil War*. New York: HarperCollins, 2006.

Wiebe, Robert H. *The Search for Order, 1877–1920*. New York: Hill and Wang, 1967.

Wiegand, Wayne A. "Tunnel Vision and Blind Spots: Reflections on the Twentieth-Century History of American Librarianship." *Library Quarterly* 69 (1999): 1–32.

Wiegand, Wayne A., and Donald G. Davis, eds. *Encyclopedia of Library History*. New York: Garland, 1994.

Williams, Raymond. *Television: Technology and Cultural Form*. New York: Schocken, 1975.

Winner, Langdon. *The Whale and the Reactor: A Search for Limits in an Age of High Technology*. Chicago: University of Chicago Press, 1986.

———. "Who Will We Be in Cyberspace?" *The Information Society* 12 (1996): 63–72.

Winseck, Dwayne R., and Robert M. Pike. *Communication and Empire: Media, Markets, and Globalization, 1860–1930*. Durham, N.C.: Duke University Press, 2007.

Winston, Brian. *Media Technology and Society: A History from the Telegraph to the Internet*. Routledge: New York, 1998.

Yates, JoAnne. *Control through Communication: The Rise of System in American Management*. Baltimore: Johns Hopkins University Press, 1989.

————. *Structuring the Information Age: Life Insurance and Technology in the Twentieth Century*. Baltimore: Johns Hopkins University Press, 2005.

Zboray, Ronald J., and Mary Saracino Zboray. *Literary Dollars and Social Sense: A People's History of the Mass Market Book*. New York: Routledge, 2005.

Zelizer, Barbie, and Stuart Allan, eds. *Journalism after September 11*. New York: Routledge, 2002.

Zook, Matthew. *The Geography of the Internet Industry*. New York: Blackwell, 2005.

Zunz, Oliver. *Making America Corporate: 1870–1920*. Chicago: University of Chicago Press, 1990.